IT Infrastructure Fundamentals: Servers, Storage, and Connectivity

James Relington

DEDICATION

To those who seek knowledge, inspiration, and new perspectives—
may this book be a companion on your journey, a spark for curiosity,
and a reminder that every page turned is a step toward discovery.

AKNOWLEDGEMENTS

I would like to express my deepest gratitude to everyone who contributed to the creation of this book. To my colleagues and mentors, your insights and expertise have been invaluable. A special thank you to my family and friends for their unwavering support and encouragement throughout this journey.

Chapter 1: Introduction to IT Infrastructure

Information Technology (IT) infrastructure is the backbone of any modern organization, providing the foundation for all technological operations. It encompasses the essential systems, hardware, software, and networking components that work together to support business processes. From powering servers to enabling communication between devices, IT infrastructure is the invisible force that makes today's digital world function. It is essential to understand what constitutes IT infrastructure and how it supports the day-to-day activities of businesses, as well as how it evolves to meet the growing demands of the digital landscape.

At its core, IT infrastructure includes a wide array of technologies. Servers are one of the most critical components, providing the processing power and storage needed to host applications, databases, and services. These servers can range from powerful machines running enterprise-level applications to smaller systems supporting less resource-intensive tasks. Alongside servers, storage systems play a crucial role in ensuring that data is securely stored and easily accessible. Whether through hard disk drives (HDDs), solid-state drives (SSDs), or more advanced technologies like Storage Area Networks (SAN), these systems allow businesses to store and retrieve vast amounts of information quickly and efficiently.

Connectivity is another essential aspect of IT infrastructure. It is the means by which servers, storage systems, and other devices communicate with each other. Networks, both local and wide area, are integral to this connectivity, enabling devices to share data, access applications, and collaborate in real-time. Network protocols, such as TCP/IP, ensure that data is transmitted reliably across these networks. Without robust networking capabilities, businesses would struggle to maintain the seamless flow of information required for modern operations. Furthermore, security is a crucial part of the IT infrastructure landscape, as protecting sensitive data and maintaining secure connections between devices is essential to prevent cyber threats and data breaches.

The evolution of IT infrastructure has been rapid, with new technologies emerging regularly. This has brought about significant changes in the way businesses manage their IT resources. Traditional on-premise infrastructure, where companies build and manage their own data centers, is gradually being supplemented – or in some cases replaced – by cloud computing. Cloud infrastructure offers businesses the ability to access and scale resources as needed, without the need to maintain physical servers and storage systems. This shift toward the cloud has transformed how organizations think about IT infrastructure, enabling greater flexibility, scalability, and cost-efficiency.

IT infrastructure is not just about the physical hardware; it also includes the software and systems that drive it. Operating systems, such as Linux and Windows Server, play a pivotal role in managing hardware resources, while applications and middleware provide the services needed for end users. The rise of virtualization technologies, where software simulates hardware, has further blurred the lines between physical and virtual infrastructure. Virtual machines and containers allow businesses to run multiple isolated environments on a single physical server, optimizing resource usage and reducing costs. Virtualization also facilitates cloud computing, enabling seamless scaling of applications and services across distributed data centers.

The growing complexity of IT infrastructure has led to the need for better management practices. As organizations adopt increasingly sophisticated technologies, they must ensure that their IT infrastructure is not only capable of supporting current needs but also flexible enough to accommodate future growth. Effective infrastructure management involves a combination of monitoring, automation, and optimization. Monitoring tools provide real-time insights into the health and performance of servers, networks, and storage systems, while automation helps streamline routine tasks such as software updates and security patches. Optimizing IT infrastructure ensures that resources are allocated efficiently, reducing waste and improving overall performance.

One of the key drivers of IT infrastructure development has been the need for businesses to keep up with the rapid pace of technological innovation. As new applications, platforms, and devices emerge, the infrastructure supporting them must evolve to ensure compatibility and efficiency. This has led to the adoption of more agile, dynamic IT systems that can quickly adapt to changing demands. Organizations must continually assess their infrastructure to identify potential bottlenecks, security vulnerabilities, and opportunities for improvement. This constant evolution is necessary to remain competitive and ensure that IT systems align with business goals.

The importance of IT infrastructure cannot be overstated. It serves as the foundation for all digital operations, enabling everything from email communication to complex data analytics. A well-designed and efficiently managed infrastructure supports business growth, innovation, and the delivery of high-quality services. As businesses increasingly rely on technology to remain competitive, the demand for robust, reliable, and scalable IT infrastructure will continue to grow. Understanding the fundamentals of IT infrastructure – from hardware components to cloud computing – is essential for anyone looking to navigate the complexities of today's technology-driven world. It allows organizations to make informed decisions about how to invest in and manage their IT resources, ensuring they are well-equipped to meet the challenges and opportunities that lie ahead.

As technology continues to evolve, the landscape of IT infrastructure will likely see further innovations. The integration of artificial intelligence (AI), machine learning, and automation into infrastructure management is expected to enhance efficiency and predictive capabilities, allowing businesses to anticipate and respond to issues before they impact operations. Similarly, the expansion of the Internet of Things (IoT) will drive the need for even more interconnected devices, further increasing the demand for scalable and resilient infrastructure. These advancements will shape the future of IT infrastructure, making it even more critical to understand its foundations and how it supports the digital world.

In summary, IT infrastructure is a dynamic and essential part of any modern organization, providing the critical components required to power digital operations. From servers and storage to networks and security, all aspects of IT infrastructure work together to ensure that businesses can run smoothly and effectively. As technology evolves, the need for advanced, flexible, and secure IT infrastructure will only increase, making it crucial for businesses to stay informed and adapt to these changes. Understanding the fundamentals of IT infrastructure is the first step in ensuring that organizations are well-equipped to handle the challenges and opportunities of the digital age.

Chapter 2: The Role of Servers in IT Infrastructure

Servers are the cornerstone of any IT infrastructure, forming the backbone of the digital ecosystem within organizations. These powerful machines are responsible for handling and managing a variety of tasks, from hosting websites and applications to storing vast amounts of data and running business-critical systems. Servers play a pivotal role in ensuring that IT infrastructure operates efficiently, reliably, and securely. Without servers, modern businesses would not be able to support the multitude of digital processes that have become essential to their operations.

At the most basic level, a server is a computer designed to process requests and deliver data to other computers over a network. Unlike personal computers, which are designed primarily for individual use, servers are built to handle multiple requests simultaneously, providing resources or services to other devices. This distinguishes them from typical desktop or laptop computers, as servers are optimized for stability, performance, and the ability to handle high workloads without interruption. Servers perform a wide range of critical tasks, including running applications, hosting databases, and managing network resources, all of which are essential to an organization's ability to function in today's fast-paced digital world.

One of the key roles of a server is hosting applications. Many business applications require a centralized platform to run on, and servers provide this platform. For instance, a web server hosts websites and serves web pages to users who access them via a browser. A database server, on the other hand, stores and manages data used by various applications within the organization. These servers are designed to support the high levels of traffic and complex queries that modern applications generate. By hosting applications on servers, organizations ensure that users can access them consistently and reliably, without the risk of overloading individual devices.

Another vital function of servers is data storage and management. In a world where data is growing at an exponential rate, efficient storage solutions are more important than ever. Servers equipped with large storage capacities enable organizations to store vast amounts of data in a secure and organized manner. This data can be anything from employee records to customer information or transactional data. A file server allows organizations to store files and documents in a centralized location, making it easier to manage and access them. Additionally, file servers can provide features such as file versioning and access control, ensuring that only authorized personnel can view or edit sensitive information.

Servers also play a critical role in managing network resources. A network server, for example, helps to facilitate communication between devices within a local area network (LAN) or wide area network (WAN). It manages and directs the flow of data between devices, ensuring that the right information reaches the right destination. A print server, for instance, allows multiple users to send print jobs to a shared printer. Similarly, a mail server handles email communication, ensuring that messages are sent, received, and stored appropriately. Servers like these are essential for maintaining seamless communication and resource sharing across an organization.

In the modern IT landscape, server virtualization has revolutionized the way servers are deployed and managed. Virtualization allows a single physical server to be divided into multiple virtual machines, each running its own operating system and applications. This technology maximizes resource utilization and reduces the need for multiple physical servers. Virtualized servers are highly flexible and can be easily scaled up or down to meet the changing demands of an organization. This scalability is particularly important in today's fast-moving business environment, where the ability to quickly adapt to new challenges and opportunities is crucial. Virtualization also enables businesses to improve their disaster recovery capabilities by allowing virtual machines to be easily backed up and restored.

Another significant advancement in server technology is the rise of cloud computing. Cloud servers are virtualized servers that are hosted in data centers and made available to organizations over the internet. These servers provide on-demand access to computing resources, such as storage, processing power, and networking, without the need for businesses to invest in and maintain their own physical infrastructure. Cloud servers have become a game-changer for organizations seeking to reduce IT overhead costs, as they eliminate the need for large upfront investments in hardware. Instead, businesses can pay for the resources they use, allowing them to scale their infrastructure in line with their needs. Cloud computing also offers the benefit of high availability and disaster recovery, as data and applications hosted in the cloud are typically distributed across multiple data centers, ensuring continuity in case of hardware failure.

The performance and reliability of servers are paramount to the smooth functioning of IT infrastructure. To ensure that servers can handle the demands placed on them, they are typically equipped with powerful processors, ample memory, and fast storage devices. These components work together to ensure that servers can handle large volumes of data and support complex operations without experiencing performance degradation. Redundancy is another key feature of server design. Many servers are built with failover mechanisms, such as redundant power supplies and hard drives, to ensure that they can continue to operate even if a component fails. This is particularly important for mission-critical systems that must be available around the clock.

Server security is another vital consideration for organizations. As servers often handle sensitive data and applications, they must be protected from unauthorized access, cyberattacks, and other security threats. Servers are typically equipped with security features such as firewalls, intrusion detection systems, and encryption technologies to safeguard data. Regular security updates and patches are essential to address vulnerabilities and protect against emerging threats. Furthermore, access to servers is typically controlled through user authentication and authorization mechanisms, ensuring that only authorized personnel can access and manage critical resources.

As organizations continue to grow and their IT needs evolve, the role of servers will become increasingly important. With the advent of new technologies such as artificial intelligence, big data analytics, and the Internet of Things (IoT), servers will need to handle more complex and data-intensive tasks. For example, AI applications often require high-performance servers equipped with specialized hardware such as graphics processing units (GPUs) to process large amounts of data quickly. Similarly, the explosion of IoT devices will create massive amounts of data that need to be processed and stored by servers in real-time. In this rapidly changing landscape, servers will remain the cornerstone of IT infrastructure, providing the power and flexibility needed to support new and emerging technologies.

Servers are indispensable to the modern IT infrastructure, playing a central role in supporting applications, managing data, and facilitating network communication. Whether in physical or virtual form, servers are the engines that drive digital operations, enabling organizations to store and process information, host critical services, and ensure seamless connectivity. As technology continues to evolve, the role of servers will remain crucial, and understanding their functions and capabilities is key to building a robust and efficient IT infrastructure. The continued advancement of server technologies will ensure that they remain at the heart of IT systems, enabling businesses to thrive in an increasingly digital world.

Chapter 3: Types of Servers and Their Functions

Servers come in various types, each serving a unique role within an organization's IT infrastructure. Understanding the different types of servers and their functions is essential for building a well-structured and efficient network. While all servers share the common purpose of delivering resources and services to other computers or devices, the specific function they perform varies based on the needs of the organization. Each type of server is optimized for specific tasks, ranging from hosting websites to managing databases and handling email communication. These specialized roles allow organizations to divide their infrastructure into distinct systems that can be managed and optimized more effectively.

The most common type of server is the file server, which is responsible for storing, managing, and sharing files across a network. File servers allow multiple users to access documents, spreadsheets, images, and other types of files from a centralized location, eliminating the need to store files on individual computers. This not only ensures that the files are easily accessible, but also improves data security and backup processes. File servers are designed to handle large volumes of data, and they can be configured to provide redundancy, ensuring that files remain available even if one part of the system fails. Access control features in file servers allow organizations to manage who can view, modify, or delete files, thus safeguarding sensitive information.

Another key type of server is the web server, which is designed to host and deliver web pages to users over the internet. Web servers use protocols like HTTP or HTTPS to serve content, such as HTML files, images, and videos, to web browsers. When a user requests a webpage by entering a URL in their browser, the request is sent to the web server, which processes the request and returns the appropriate content. Web servers are integral to the operation of websites, applications, and online services, and they are often optimized to handle high volumes of traffic. To ensure high availability and performance, web servers are often deployed in clusters, allowing for load balancing and failover mechanisms that distribute requests across multiple servers.

In addition to file and web servers, database servers play a critical role in managing and storing data for applications and services. A database server is designed to run database management systems (DBMS), which are used to store, organize, and query data. Database servers are essential for managing structured data, such as customer records, inventory information, and financial data. These servers are typically optimized for performance, as they need to handle complex queries and large volumes of data. Database servers also provide features like data integrity, backup, and recovery, ensuring that critical information is stored securely and remains accessible even in the event of system failures.

Another important category of servers is the mail server, which manages the sending, receiving, and storage of email messages. Mail servers are responsible for ensuring that emails are delivered to the correct recipient, whether within the same organization or externally. They use protocols like SMTP (Simple Mail Transfer Protocol), POP3 (Post Office Protocol), and IMAP (Internet Message Access Protocol) to send and retrieve emails. Mail servers can be configured to handle both incoming and outgoing emails, and they often include features such as spam filtering, encryption, and access control to protect against unauthorized access and to ensure secure communication. They are a crucial part of any organization's communication infrastructure, providing a reliable and efficient means for employees to exchange information.

In a modern network, application servers are increasingly important. These servers are used to host and run software applications that provide specific services to users. An application server acts as an intermediary between the client (user's device) and the underlying resources, processing requests and managing the logic of the application. For example, an e-commerce platform might use an application server to handle transactions, manage inventory, and provide users with real-time data. Application servers can be configured to support multiple applications, making them versatile tools for businesses with a diverse range of software needs. They also often integrate with other types of servers, such as database servers, to provide a complete solution.

The print server is another specialized server that plays an important role in managing print devices within a network. Print servers allow multiple users to share a single printer, ensuring that print jobs are sent to the correct device without requiring each user to be directly connected to the printer. These servers are particularly useful in environments with numerous users, such as offices and schools, where many people need access to printing resources. Print servers can manage multiple printers, providing centralized control over the printing process. They also allow administrators to monitor printer status, queue print jobs, and manage user access to printing resources.

Proxy servers are another type of server that acts as an intermediary between a user and the internet. When a user requests data from the internet, the request is first routed through the proxy server, which then fetches the data on behalf of the user. This process can improve security, as the proxy server can filter requests to prevent malicious content from reaching the user. Proxy servers are often used in corporate environments to restrict access to certain websites, protect against cyber threats, and improve network performance by caching frequently accessed content. They can also provide anonymity for users by masking their IP addresses.

The DNS (Domain Name System) server is responsible for translating human-readable domain names (such as www.example.com) into IP addresses, which are used by computers to identify each other on the network. DNS servers play a fundamental role in the functioning of the internet, as they enable users to access websites using easy-to-remember domain names instead of complicated numerical IP addresses. These servers work by maintaining a database of domain names and their corresponding IP addresses, allowing them to quickly resolve requests and direct users to the appropriate destination.

Game servers are another type of server that has gained popularity in recent years, particularly with the rise of online multiplayer gaming. Game servers host video games that players connect to over the internet, allowing them to play together in real-time. These servers provide the infrastructure needed to synchronize game data, such as player positions and actions, ensuring that all participants experience the game in the same way. Game servers must be able to handle large volumes of simultaneous connections and provide low-latency performance to ensure a smooth gaming experience.

In large organizations, enterprise servers are used to support a wide variety of business applications and services. These high-performance servers are designed to handle the complex and demanding workloads of large-scale operations. Enterprise servers are often equipped with specialized hardware and software to support multiple virtual machines and manage extensive data storage needs. They are typically deployed in data centers and are critical to maintaining the operations of large organizations, providing everything from internal communication tools to customer-facing services.

Each type of server plays a vital role in the larger IT ecosystem of an organization. By distributing tasks across different server types, organizations can create an efficient, scalable, and reliable infrastructure that supports their diverse needs. Whether hosting files, managing databases, or ensuring secure communication, servers form the foundation of modern IT operations. The variety of server types available allows organizations to customize their infrastructure to meet specific requirements, ensuring that each function is handled by the most appropriate technology. As the digital world continues to evolve, so too will the roles and functions of servers, ensuring their continued importance in the success of businesses and organizations across the globe.

Chapter 4: Server Hardware: Components and Specifications

The hardware that makes up a server is fundamental to its performance, reliability, and scalability. Unlike personal computers or laptops, servers are designed with specific components that prioritize durability, power efficiency, and the ability to handle multiple tasks simultaneously. When selecting or designing a server, understanding the components and specifications that contribute to its function is essential for ensuring it can meet the demands of the organization it serves. These components work together to provide the computational power, storage capacity, and network connectivity that are required for modern IT infrastructure.

At the heart of every server is the central processing unit (CPU). The CPU, often referred to as the server's brain, is responsible for executing instructions and processing data. Server CPUs are typically more powerful and more reliable than those found in personal computers, as they need to handle complex operations and multiple tasks at once. Server processors often have multiple cores, allowing them to process several threads simultaneously, which improves performance, particularly in environments where multitasking is critical. CPUs designed for servers, such as Intel Xeon or AMD EPYC processors, are engineered for stability and longevity, ensuring that servers can operate continuously without failure.

Another key component of server hardware is memory, or RAM (Random Access Memory). RAM is used by the server to temporarily store data that is actively being used or processed. The amount of memory in a server is critical because it determines how much data can be accessed and manipulated at once, affecting the server's overall speed and responsiveness. Servers typically require more RAM than desktop computers, as they often need to support many simultaneous users and complex applications. Memory modules used in servers are designed for higher reliability and error correction, often incorporating technologies like ECC (Error-Correcting Code) memory, which helps prevent data corruption by detecting and correcting common types of memory errors.

Equally important is the storage system in a server. Servers typically require large amounts of storage to hold data, applications, and user files. Unlike consumer-grade systems that use a single hard drive or solid-state drive (SSD), servers are often equipped with multiple drives configured in various RAID (Redundant Array of Independent Disks) configurations to provide redundancy, fault tolerance, and improved performance. The storage in servers is usually designed to be scalable, meaning that additional storage can be added as needed to accommodate growing data needs. Servers can use a variety of storage technologies, such as HDDs (hard disk drives) for large, cost-effective storage or SSDs for faster, more reliable performance. The choice of storage media depends on the specific requirements of the server, including speed, capacity, and budget.

The motherboard is the backbone that connects all the server's components, ensuring they can communicate with each other. A server motherboard is typically larger and more robust than those found in personal computers, designed to support multiple processors, large amounts of memory, and various types of expansion cards. The motherboard includes several slots for additional components such as network interface cards (NICs) and graphics processing units (GPUs), which may be added to enhance the server's capabilities. It also houses critical components like the system chipset, which controls data flow between the CPU, memory, and other components.

To ensure that servers can handle high levels of traffic and continuous workloads, they require power supplies that are both reliable and efficient. Unlike consumer PCs, which may have a single power supply, servers often have redundant power supplies to ensure that the system remains operational even if one power supply fails. These power supplies are typically designed to meet the stringent requirements of data centers, where uptime is critical. Power efficiency is also a key concern, and many modern server power supplies are designed to meet energy-efficient standards, reducing operational costs and the environmental impact of running large server farms.

Cooling systems are another vital aspect of server hardware. Servers generate a significant amount of heat due to the intensive processing tasks they perform. Overheating can lead to system instability, reduced performance, and even hardware failure. To prevent this, servers are equipped with advanced cooling solutions, including fans, heat sinks, and liquid cooling systems. These systems are designed to maintain optimal operating temperatures, even under heavy loads. In data centers, where thousands of servers are running simultaneously, specialized cooling technologies are used to manage the heat generated by so many devices. Proper cooling ensures the longevity and reliability of server hardware.

Networking capabilities are also a critical component of server hardware. Servers need to be able to communicate with other devices on the network, whether it be within the local area network (LAN) or over the internet. This is achieved through network interface cards (NICs), which allow the server to send and receive data over the network. Servers often have multiple NICs for redundancy and performance reasons, enabling them to handle high volumes of network traffic. For example, a web server might have multiple NICs to balance incoming traffic, ensuring that no single connection becomes overwhelmed. High-speed NICs, capable of supporting Gigabit or even 10-Gigabit Ethernet, are commonly used in servers to ensure fast and reliable communication.

For some specialized tasks, servers may also include graphics processing units (GPUs). While not typically required for most server functions, GPUs are becoming increasingly important in certain fields, such as artificial intelligence (AI) and machine learning (ML), where large-scale parallel processing is needed. GPUs excel at handling multiple operations simultaneously, making them ideal for workloads that involve processing large amounts of data in parallel. Many modern servers, particularly those designed for data analytics, scientific research, or AI, come equipped with specialized GPU cards that accelerate performance for these types of tasks.

Lastly, expandability is a crucial factor in server hardware. As business needs grow, servers often need to be upgraded or expanded to handle increased workloads. Many servers are designed with this in mind, offering modular components that can be upgraded without replacing the entire system. For example, additional memory modules, storage drives, or network cards can be added as needed. This expandability ensures that servers can scale with the organization's needs, providing a cost-effective way to accommodate growing demands.

The rack-mounted form factor is another specification that plays a significant role in server hardware. In large data centers, servers are often installed in racks, which are standard units that allow for efficient use of space. Rack-mounted servers are designed to fit into these racks, which can house multiple servers in a compact and organized manner. This form factor allows for easy access to each server, as well as efficient airflow and cooling management. Servers designed for rack mounting typically have a slim profile and are built to be highly durable and easy to maintain.

The hardware components and specifications of a server are critical to its performance and the ability to support the needs of the organization. From the CPU and memory to storage and network connectivity, each piece of hardware plays a vital role in ensuring that the server can handle its intended tasks efficiently. By carefully selecting the right hardware, organizations can build servers that not only meet their current requirements but are also flexible enough to grow with their future needs. Understanding these components is essential for anyone involved in the design, deployment, and management of IT infrastructure, as it ensures that servers perform optimally and continue to deliver reliable service over time.

Chapter 5: Operating Systems for Servers

The operating system (OS) is one of the most critical components of server infrastructure. It serves as the intermediary between the hardware and the software applications that run on a server. Without an operating system, a server would be unable to function, as it would lack the necessary environment to manage hardware resources, handle network communication, and execute tasks. Server operating systems are specifically designed to optimize performance, reliability, and security, allowing servers to handle demanding workloads and support the critical functions required by businesses and organizations. These operating systems must be robust enough to ensure that the server operates continuously, even under high levels of stress, without compromising performance or stability.

One of the primary roles of a server operating system is to manage the server's hardware resources. The OS is responsible for allocating the server's central processing unit (CPU), memory, storage, and network interfaces to the various processes that run on the server. It must ensure that resources are used efficiently, allowing multiple processes to run simultaneously without interfering with each other. Additionally, the operating system provides a platform for running server applications, such as web servers, database servers, and email servers, enabling them to function properly and interact with other systems on the network.

When it comes to server operating systems, the two dominant options are Linux and Windows Server, each offering a range of benefits depending on the needs of the organization. Linux-based operating systems, such as Ubuntu Server, CentOS, and Red Hat Enterprise Linux (RHEL), are popular choices for many organizations due to their stability, scalability, and open-source nature. Being open-source means that Linux distributions are freely available and can be customized to meet specific needs, which makes them highly versatile. Linux also has a reputation for being highly secure, with a large community of developers constantly monitoring and patching vulnerabilities. Its flexibility and configurability make it ideal for environments where performance, security, and cost-effectiveness are top priorities.

Linux-based server operating systems are also known for their strong support of web hosting and cloud infrastructure. Many web servers, like Apache and Nginx, are optimized for Linux environments, providing reliable and efficient solutions for hosting websites and applications. Additionally, Linux is widely used in cloud computing environments due to its ability to scale efficiently, making it a popular choice for large-scale deployments, especially in virtualized environments. The flexibility of Linux allows administrators to configure the system exactly how they need it, which is particularly important in complex server environments where fine-grained control is required.

On the other hand, Windows Server is a proprietary operating system developed by Microsoft, and it is commonly used in businesses that rely on Microsoft products and services. Windows Server offers a user-friendly interface that makes it easier for administrators to manage and configure the server, which can be particularly useful in environments where IT staff may not be as familiar with command-line interfaces. It also provides deep integration with other Microsoft products, such as Active Directory, Microsoft Exchange, and Microsoft SQL Server, making it an ideal choice for organizations that use these tools for their business operations. Windows Server is also known for its strong support for enterprise applications and its ability to integrate seamlessly with existing Microsoft environments, offering high levels of compatibility and support for a wide range of applications.

One of the key strengths of Windows Server is its ability to support various types of workloads, including file sharing, printing, and remote access, all within a single integrated environment. The server's built-in tools, such as the Server Manager and Windows Admin Center, simplify the management of these services, making it easier for administrators to configure and monitor servers. Additionally, Windows Server supports Hyper-V, Microsoft's virtualization technology, which allows administrators to create and manage virtual machines (VMs) on a single physical server. This is particularly beneficial in environments that require high availability and scalability, as virtualization allows for better resource utilization and easy deployment of multiple virtual instances.

While Linux and Windows Server are the most widely used server operating systems, there are other options available, each with its own advantages. UNIX operating systems, such as AIX, HP-UX, and Solaris, have been used in enterprise environments for decades. While UNIX-based systems are not as commonly deployed as Linux or Windows Server, they are known for their stability and reliability, making them a strong choice for mission-critical applications, especially in industries like telecommunications and financial services. UNIX systems are optimized for high-performance computing, and they offer advanced security features, making them suitable for environments that demand the highest levels of reliability and uptime.

Another type of server operating system gaining popularity is BSD (Berkeley Software Distribution), which includes operating systems like FreeBSD, OpenBSD, and NetBSD. BSD-based systems are known for their performance, security, and licensing model, which is less restrictive than Linux. These operating systems are commonly used in specialized environments that require a high level of customization and control. FreeBSD, for example, is often chosen for networking and storage solutions, where its advanced networking capabilities and performance features make it an ideal choice. OpenBSD, on the other hand, is particularly known for its focus on security, with a strong emphasis on code correctness and vulnerability prevention.

As businesses increasingly turn to cloud computing and virtualization for their IT infrastructure needs, the operating systems used in these environments have also evolved. In cloud environments, servers need to be able to handle dynamic workloads, scale efficiently, and provide high availability. Both Linux and Windows Server are commonly used in cloud environments, but cloud service providers like Amazon Web Services (AWS), Google Cloud Platform (GCP), and Microsoft Azure offer their own customized versions of server operating systems optimized for their specific platforms. These cloud-specific operating systems are designed to integrate seamlessly with cloud-based tools and services, allowing organizations to take advantage of the scalability and flexibility of cloud computing.

Server operating systems must also include robust security features, as servers are often exposed to a wide range of security threats, including unauthorized access, malware, and data breaches. Modern server operating systems come with built-in security features such as firewalls, intrusion detection systems, and encryption tools. For example, Windows Server includes Windows Defender, a built-in antivirus and anti-malware solution, while Linux distributions typically offer a variety of open-source security tools, such as iptables for firewall management and SELinux for enhanced access control. Security updates and patches are essential to maintaining the integrity of the operating system, and many server OSs include tools for automating updates and managing vulnerabilities.

The choice of server operating system depends on the specific needs of the organization, including factors such as cost, security, scalability, and the existing IT infrastructure. Each server operating system offers a different set of features and capabilities, making it important for administrators to carefully consider the requirements of their environment before making a decision. Whether opting for a Linux-based solution, a Windows Server deployment, or a more specialized UNIX or BSD system, the operating system is a fundamental piece of the server's architecture, influencing its performance, security, and ability to support the organization's needs.

Chapter 6: Server Virtualization and Hypervisors

Server virtualization is a technology that has revolutionized the way organizations manage their IT infrastructure. It allows for the creation of virtual instances of servers, enabling multiple operating systems to run on a single physical machine. This process significantly enhances the efficiency, scalability, and flexibility of server management, while also reducing costs associated with hardware procurement and maintenance. Server virtualization uses a layer of software known as a hypervisor to create and manage these virtual environments, ensuring that each virtual machine (VM) operates independently while sharing the resources of the physical server. The introduction of virtualization has been one of the most transformative changes in IT infrastructure, empowering businesses to streamline operations, optimize resource usage, and improve system availability.

At its core, server virtualization allows one physical server to run several virtual machines, each of which acts as an independent server. Each virtual machine is capable of running its own operating system and applications, and it behaves as though it is running on a physical server. This is made possible by a hypervisor, which is a specialized piece of software that manages the virtual environments and allocates physical resources like CPU, memory, storage, and networking to each VM. The hypervisor sits between the physical hardware and the virtual machines, ensuring that the VMs remain isolated from each other while still sharing the underlying resources of the host machine.

Hypervisors are the fundamental technology behind server virtualization, and they come in two main types: Type 1 and Type 2. A Type 1 hypervisor, also known as a bare-metal hypervisor, is installed directly on the physical hardware of the server. This type of hypervisor does not require a host operating system because it runs directly on the server hardware, making it more efficient and secure. Examples of Type 1 hypervisors include VMware vSphere/ESXi, Microsoft Hyper-V, and XenServer. These hypervisors are commonly used in data centers and enterprise environments due to their performance, scalability, and ability to handle large numbers of virtual machines.

A Type 2 hypervisor, on the other hand, runs on top of an existing operating system. This means that it relies on the host operating system for access to hardware resources. Type 2 hypervisors are often used for development, testing, and small-scale environments where the overhead of a Type 1 hypervisor is not necessary. Examples of Type 2 hypervisors include VMware Workstation and Oracle VirtualBox. While Type 2 hypervisors offer greater ease of use and flexibility, they do not perform as well as Type 1 hypervisors when it comes to managing large, high-performance workloads.

One of the primary benefits of server virtualization is the consolidation of resources. In traditional server environments, each physical server is often dedicated to a single task or application. This can lead to underutilization of hardware resources, as some servers may only use a small portion of their available CPU, memory, or storage. Virtualization solves this problem by allowing multiple virtual machines to share the resources of a single physical server. This leads to higher server utilization and a more efficient use of hardware. In many cases, server virtualization can reduce the need for additional physical servers, leading to savings in hardware, energy consumption, and physical space within the data center.

Another significant advantage of server virtualization is its flexibility. Virtual machines are highly portable and can be moved between different physical servers with minimal disruption to the underlying services. This allows for easier load balancing, disaster recovery, and maintenance. For example, if a physical server needs to be taken offline for maintenance, the virtual machines running on that server can be quickly migrated to another physical server in the environment, ensuring that there is no downtime. This level of flexibility also extends to scalability. As the needs of the organization grow, new virtual machines can be provisioned on demand, without the need for additional physical hardware. This makes it easier to scale infrastructure quickly and efficiently, without the need for lengthy procurement and deployment processes.

Server virtualization also provides significant improvements in disaster recovery and business continuity. Virtual machines are typically stored as files, which means they can be backed up, cloned, and restored with relative ease. This makes it possible to quickly replicate virtual machines to remote locations or cloud environments, ensuring that critical services can be restored quickly in the event of a disaster. Additionally, the use of snapshots—point-in-time copies of virtual machines—allows administrators to quickly roll back to a known good configuration if something goes wrong with an application or system update. This level of data protection and recovery is much more efficient and cost-effective than traditional physical server backup methods.

The management of virtualized environments is another area where hypervisors play a crucial role. Hypervisors come with powerful management tools that allow IT administrators to monitor and control the virtual machines running on the server. These management tools provide features such as resource allocation, performance monitoring, and capacity planning, making it easier to ensure that the virtual machines are operating efficiently and that resources are being distributed appropriately. In larger environments, virtualization management tools, such as VMware vCenter, Microsoft System Center Virtual Machine Manager, and Red Hat Virtualization, provide centralized control over multiple hypervisors and virtual machines, enabling administrators to automate many of the routine tasks associated with managing virtualized infrastructure.

Despite the many benefits of server virtualization, there are also challenges that need to be addressed. Performance overhead is one such challenge. While virtualization enables efficient resource sharing, it also introduces some overhead, as the hypervisor itself consumes resources to manage the virtual machines. This can sometimes result in a slight reduction in performance compared to running applications directly on physical hardware. However, advancements in hypervisor technology and the increasing power of modern hardware have minimized these performance impacts in most cases.

Another challenge is security. Virtualized environments can be more complex to secure, as each virtual machine runs its own operating system and may have different security requirements. Additionally, the hypervisor itself becomes a critical point of failure. If the hypervisor is compromised, all virtual machines running on that host are at risk. It is essential for organizations to implement strong security practices, including network segmentation, access control, and regular security updates, to protect their virtualized environments.

Server virtualization has fundamentally changed the way organizations deploy, manage, and scale their IT infrastructure. By using hypervisors to create multiple virtual machines on a single physical server, organizations can improve resource utilization, enhance scalability, and streamline disaster recovery. The flexibility and cost savings offered by server virtualization make it a powerful tool for modern IT environments, and its impact on server management will continue to grow as technology advances. The use of hypervisors as a critical component of server virtualization ensures that organizations can take full advantage of the benefits of virtualization while maintaining control over their infrastructure and ensuring that it remains efficient, secure, and scalable.

Chapter 7: Server Storage: Introduction and Basics

Server storage is one of the most critical components of any IT infrastructure. It is the system that manages the storage, retrieval, and organization of data on a server. In the context of modern IT environments, where data is continually growing and becoming more complex, server storage plays a pivotal role in ensuring that organizations can access, protect, and manage their data effectively. The growing reliance on data-intensive applications, virtualized environments, and cloud services has placed increasing demands on storage systems, making it essential for organizations to carefully plan and manage their server storage infrastructure to meet these needs.

At its most basic level, server storage refers to the devices and technologies used to store digital data on a server. Unlike desktop computers, where storage typically consists of a single hard disk drive (HDD) or solid-state drive (SSD), server storage systems are much more complex and are designed to meet the demands of multiple users and applications. Servers may require large amounts of storage space to handle the data needs of enterprise-level applications, file sharing, databases, and backup systems. To meet these requirements, server storage can involve various technologies, architectures, and configurations, all of which are designed to provide speed, reliability, and scalability.

One of the most fundamental aspects of server storage is the type of storage media used. Traditionally, servers have relied on hard disk drives (HDDs) for storage. These mechanical drives use spinning disks to read and write data, making them relatively inexpensive and capable of storing large amounts of data. However, HDDs are slower than solid-state drives (SSDs), which have become increasingly popular in server environments. SSDs, which use flash memory to store data, offer significantly faster data access times, reduced power consumption, and greater durability compared to HDDs. As a result, SSDs are often used for high-performance applications where speed is critical, such as databases, web servers, and virtualization environments. The decision to use HDDs or SSDs depends on factors such as performance requirements, budget, and storage capacity.

In addition to the storage media itself, server storage often involves complex architectures designed to provide redundancy, scalability, and performance. One of the most common methods of achieving redundancy and performance is through the use of RAID (Redundant Array of Independent Disks) technology. RAID combines multiple physical hard drives or SSDs into a single logical unit, offering various configurations that balance speed, data protection, and storage capacity. For example, RAID 1 uses mirroring to create an exact copy of data on two separate drives, providing redundancy in case one drive fails. RAID 5, on the other hand, uses striping with parity, distributing data across multiple drives while also providing fault tolerance. By using RAID, servers can increase data reliability and performance, ensuring that data is not lost in the event of hardware failure.

Beyond RAID, server storage often involves Storage Area Networks (SANs) and Network Attached Storage (NAS) systems. A SAN is a high-performance, dedicated network of storage devices that are connected to servers, allowing them to access large amounts of data quickly. SANs are typically used in environments where high availability, fast data access, and centralized management are essential, such as in data centers or virtualized environments. SANs provide high-speed connections between storage devices and servers, ensuring that large datasets can be accessed with minimal latency. They are also highly scalable, making them an ideal choice for organizations that need to grow their storage infrastructure as data demands increase.

In contrast, a NAS system is a storage device that is connected to a network, allowing multiple servers or users to access files and data over the network. NAS is typically used for file-based storage, where multiple users need to access shared files and documents. Unlike SANs, which operate at the block level, NAS operates at the file level, meaning that users access files directly over the network. NAS systems are easy to set up and manage, making them an attractive option for businesses that require simple, cost-effective file storage without the complexity of a SAN. While NAS does not offer the same performance as a SAN, it is an excellent solution for small to medium-sized businesses that need to store and share files across multiple users and applications.

As server environments become more complex, the demand for scalability in storage solutions has increased. Organizations need storage systems that can easily grow with their needs, especially as data volumes continue to expand. One of the ways to achieve scalability is through storage virtualization, which allows storage resources to be pooled and managed as a single entity, regardless of the underlying hardware. Storage virtualization enables administrators to allocate and manage storage more efficiently, as they can easily add or remove storage devices without affecting the overall system. This flexibility allows organizations to respond quickly to changing data storage needs, reducing the time and effort required to scale the infrastructure.

Cloud storage has also become an important part of server storage in recent years. Cloud storage allows organizations to store data off-site, providing additional flexibility and scalability. With cloud storage, businesses no longer need to invest heavily in physical storage devices or worry about managing the infrastructure themselves. Instead, they can use third-party providers, such as Amazon Web Services (AWS), Microsoft Azure, or Google Cloud, to store and access their data remotely. Cloud storage offers several advantages, including cost savings, easy access from anywhere, and automatic backups. However, it also presents challenges, such as data security, compliance, and bandwidth limitations, which organizations need to consider when incorporating cloud storage into their overall infrastructure.

In addition to the physical storage systems and technologies, server storage involves the management and organization of data. Data management is crucial to ensure that data is stored securely, accessed efficiently, and backed up regularly. Storage management tools are used to monitor the health of storage systems, track performance, and allocate resources appropriately. These tools allow administrators to set up automated backups, implement disaster recovery strategies, and ensure that data is available when needed. Effective data management is essential for preventing data loss, improving system performance, and maintaining regulatory compliance, particularly for organizations that store sensitive or critical information.

The security of server storage is also a top priority. As servers often house sensitive data, such as customer information, financial records, and intellectual property, it is essential to implement strong security measures to protect this data. Encryption is one of the most common techniques used to safeguard data at rest and in transit. By encrypting the data stored on servers, businesses can ensure that even if the storage media is compromised, the data remains secure. Additionally, access controls and authentication mechanisms must be implemented to ensure that only authorized users can access sensitive storage resources.

As the volume and complexity of data continue to grow, server storage systems will need to evolve to meet the changing demands of businesses and organizations. The use of SSDs, advanced RAID configurations, SANs, NAS, and cloud storage will continue to play an essential role in ensuring that data is stored, accessed, and protected efficiently. By leveraging these technologies and implementing effective data management and security practices, organizations can build server storage systems that meet the needs of modern IT environments. Server storage is not just about providing space for data, but about ensuring that data is available, secure, and optimized for the demands of today's digital world.

Chapter 8: Understanding Storage Architectures

Storage architecture refers to the design and organization of the various components and systems that store and manage data in an IT infrastructure. As businesses and organizations rely more heavily on data, understanding storage architectures has become a fundamental aspect of IT planning and management. Effective storage architectures are essential for optimizing performance, ensuring data availability, and maintaining the reliability of systems. The way data is structured, stored, and accessed can significantly impact the overall performance and scalability of an organization's IT infrastructure. With the increasing need for efficient data management, organizations must make informed decisions about how to structure their storage systems to meet both current and future needs.

At the heart of any storage architecture is the concept of data storage devices. These devices can vary in form and function, ranging from traditional hard disk drives (HDDs) to the more modern solid-state drives (SSDs). While HDDs remain a cost-effective solution for bulk storage, SSDs are favored for high-performance environments due to their faster read and write speeds. The combination of these two types of storage, often used together in a tiered architecture, allows businesses to balance cost and performance. Storage devices are organized into storage arrays, which are collections of disks managed as a single unit. These arrays can be configured in various ways to optimize performance, fault tolerance, and data redundancy.

One of the most critical aspects of storage architecture is the data access method. The most common methods for accessing data are file-level and block-level storage. File-level storage is used in systems where data is stored in a hierarchical structure of directories and files. This method is ideal for applications that require shared access to data, such as document management systems or file servers. Block-level storage, on the other hand, organizes data into fixed-size blocks and allows data to be read or written in blocks rather than as whole files. This method is typically used for applications that require high performance and low latency, such as databases and virtualized environments. Understanding the difference between file-level and block-level storage is essential when designing a storage architecture, as it helps determine how data will be stored, accessed, and managed within the system.

Storage architectures can be further categorized into three main types: direct-attached storage (DAS), network-attached storage (NAS), and storage area networks (SAN). DAS refers to storage devices that are directly attached to a single server or workstation, typically via internal hard drives or external USB drives. While DAS is simple and inexpensive, it has limitations in terms of scalability and data sharing. It is best suited for small-scale environments or individual workstations that do not require centralized data access. In contrast, NAS is a file-level storage architecture that provides centralized storage accessible over a network. NAS devices typically use Ethernet to connect to the network, allowing multiple servers or users to access the stored data. NAS is an ideal solution for environments where file sharing and collaboration are important, such as in offices or small to medium-sized businesses.

SAN, on the other hand, is a high-performance, block-level storage network that provides access to storage devices across multiple servers. SANs are typically used in large-scale data centers or enterprise environments where performance, redundancy, and scalability are critical. A SAN is designed to allow servers to access storage resources as if they were locally attached, providing faster data access speeds and enabling large-scale data management. SANs are often implemented using fiber channel or iSCSI (Internet Small Computer Systems Interface) protocols, which ensure high-speed, low-latency connections between storage devices and servers. The primary advantage of SANs is their ability to consolidate storage resources, allowing for greater flexibility and scalability in managing large volumes of data.

In addition to DAS, NAS, and SAN, modern storage architectures often include virtualization to further enhance the flexibility and scalability of storage systems. Storage virtualization involves abstracting the physical storage hardware from the software applications that use it, creating a virtual layer that allows for more efficient management and provisioning of storage resources. This technology enables administrators to pool storage from multiple devices, creating a unified storage environment that can be managed as a single entity. Storage virtualization also allows for the creation of virtual storage pools, which can be dynamically allocated to applications as needed, ensuring optimal resource utilization. This is particularly important in environments where data storage needs are constantly changing, such as in cloud computing or virtualized environments.

Cloud storage has become an increasingly important component of modern storage architectures, offering scalability and flexibility that traditional storage systems cannot match. In cloud storage, data is stored off-site in remote data centers and accessed over the internet. Cloud storage services, such as Amazon Web Services (AWS), Microsoft Azure, and Google Cloud, provide businesses with the ability to scale their storage needs on-demand, paying only for the storage they use. This has significant cost advantages, as businesses no longer need to invest in and maintain expensive physical storage infrastructure. Cloud storage also provides enhanced redundancy and disaster recovery capabilities, as data is typically stored across multiple data centers in different geographic locations. However, cloud storage does come with concerns about security, data privacy, and compliance, making it important for businesses to carefully evaluate their storage requirements before transitioning to the cloud.

The design of storage architecture must also take into account data protection and security. As data becomes increasingly valuable, protecting it from loss, corruption, and unauthorized access is critical. Storage architectures often include built-in redundancy features, such as RAID configurations, to protect against hardware failures. For example, RAID 1 mirrors data across two disks, ensuring that if one disk fails, the data is still available on the other. RAID 5 uses striping with parity to provide both performance and redundancy, allowing for data recovery in the event of a single disk failure. In addition to RAID, backup systems and disaster recovery strategies are integral components of a storage architecture, ensuring that data can be restored in the event of a system failure or data loss.

Encryption is another critical element in securing stored data. By encrypting data both at rest and in transit, organizations can ensure that even if their storage systems are compromised, the data will remain secure. Encryption protects sensitive information from unauthorized access, ensuring compliance with regulatory requirements and safeguarding business-critical data. Storage systems can be configured to automatically encrypt data, both on local storage devices and when it is transferred over the network or to the cloud.

The scalability of a storage architecture is a critical consideration, particularly in environments where data volumes are growing rapidly. Modern storage systems are designed to scale easily, allowing organizations to add additional storage capacity as needed without significant disruptions to ongoing operations. This scalability is achieved through a combination of virtualization, modular storage units, and cloud storage integration. Organizations can expand their storage capacity incrementally, ensuring that they only pay for the storage they need at any given time.

As data continues to grow in volume and complexity, the design of storage architectures will continue to evolve. Innovations such as software-defined storage (SDS), where the storage management layer is decoupled from the physical hardware, will provide even greater flexibility and efficiency in managing data. SDS allows organizations to manage storage resources across multiple platforms, whether on-premises, in the cloud, or in hybrid environments. As the need for high availability, low latency, and rapid access to data intensifies, organizations will need to continue to refine their storage architectures to ensure that they can meet these demands efficiently and securely. The goal will always be to provide a storage solution that is not only cost-effective and scalable but also resilient and optimized for the needs of modern businesses.

Chapter 9: Disk Drives: HDDs vs. SSDs

Disk drives are fundamental components in the storage architecture of servers, desktops, and virtually all other computing devices. They are the primary means of storing data, including operating systems, applications, files, and databases. Over the years, two primary types of disk drives have emerged as the most widely used storage solutions: Hard Disk Drives (HDDs) and Solid-State Drives (SSDs). While both serve the same purpose of providing storage, they differ significantly in terms of their internal mechanisms, performance, durability, and suitability for different applications. Understanding the strengths and weaknesses of HDDs and SSDs is crucial for making informed decisions about which type of storage to implement in a given IT infrastructure.

Hard Disk Drives (HDDs) are the traditional storage solution that has been used in computing for decades. They rely on mechanical components, primarily a spinning disk and a read/write head, to store and retrieve data. The disk is coated with a magnetic material that allows the read/write head to magnetize tiny areas of the disk, representing binary data. As the disk spins at high speeds, the read/write head moves over the surface of the disk to access the data stored in specific sectors. The mechanical nature of HDDs makes them relatively slower compared to newer technologies like SSDs, but they have historically been favored for their cost-effectiveness and large storage capacities.

One of the key advantages of HDDs is their cost per gigabyte, which remains significantly lower than that of SSDs. This makes HDDs an attractive option for scenarios where large amounts of storage are required without the need for ultra-fast data access. For example, HDDs are commonly used in personal computers, data backup systems, and high-capacity storage arrays where speed is not as critical as the amount of data being stored. Additionally, HDDs are available in a wide range of capacities, making them suitable for both consumer-grade and enterprise-level storage needs. As a result, HDDs continue to be widely used despite the growing popularity of SSDs.

However, the mechanical components of HDDs also present a number of limitations. The moving parts in an HDD, particularly the spinning disk and the read/write arm, are prone to wear and tear over time. As the drive ages, it becomes more susceptible to mechanical failure, which can result in data loss or corruption. Furthermore, the speed of data retrieval is limited by the rotational speed of the disk, typically measured in revolutions per minute (RPM). Common speeds for consumer-grade HDDs range from 5,400 RPM to 7,200 RPM, with higher-end drives reaching speeds of up to 10,000 RPM or more. While this is sufficient for many applications, it does not compare to the speed offered by SSDs, which have no moving parts and can access data almost instantaneously.

Solid-State Drives (SSDs), on the other hand, represent a more modern storage technology that has become increasingly popular in recent years. Instead of using mechanical components, SSDs rely on flash memory chips to store data. These chips are made up of memory cells that retain data even when power is turned off, which is a key characteristic of non-volatile memory. The absence of moving parts allows SSDs to offer significant improvements in performance, reliability, and durability over traditional HDDs. The data access speed of an SSD is much faster, as the drive can access any location on the memory chip instantly, without the need for mechanical movement or waiting for a disk to spin.

One of the primary advantages of SSDs is their speed. The read and write speeds of an SSD are far superior to those of an HDD, making them ideal for tasks that require fast data access, such as running operating systems, applications, and databases. SSDs can drastically reduce boot times, application load times, and data transfer speeds, which makes them particularly advantageous for environments where high performance is required, such as in servers, gaming systems, and high-performance computing. For example, an SSD can typically achieve read speeds of over 500 MB/s, while high-end models can reach speeds exceeding 3,000 MB/s with the use of the NVMe (Non-Volatile Memory Express) protocol, which is much faster than the typical transfer rates of HDDs.

In addition to speed, SSDs offer reliability and durability that HDDs cannot match. Because SSDs have no moving parts, they are less prone to mechanical failure. This makes them more robust in environments that involve frequent vibrations, shocks, or movement. As a result, SSDs are often the preferred choice for mobile devices like laptops and smartphones, where durability is essential. The absence of moving parts also means that SSDs generate less heat and consume less power compared to HDDs, which makes them more energy-efficient and suitable for use in data centers and systems where power consumption is a concern.

Despite these advantages, SSDs also have their own set of limitations. The most notable is the cost. SSDs are still more expensive per gigabyte compared to HDDs, although the price difference has been steadily decreasing as SSD technology advances and becomes more widely adopted. For users or organizations that require large amounts of storage, the cost of SSDs can be prohibitive. While SSD prices continue to fall, for applications that need massive storage at a lower cost, HDDs remain the more economical choice. Moreover, SSDs have a limited number of write cycles. Flash memory cells in SSDs degrade over time with repeated writes, which can reduce the lifespan of the drive. While modern SSDs have significantly improved in terms of write endurance, they still do not match the lifespan of an HDD under heavy write-intensive workloads.

Another factor to consider is storage capacity. While SSDs are available in large capacities, the cost of high-capacity SSDs is still significantly higher than that of equivalent HDDs. For applications that require many terabytes of storage, such as video editing or large-scale data storage, HDDs may still be the preferred option due to their lower cost per terabyte. However, for applications where speed and performance are critical, such as database servers or high-performance computing environments, the benefits of SSDs typically outweigh the higher cost.

The decision between choosing an HDD or an SSD depends on the specific requirements of the application or system in question. For users who prioritize cost-effectiveness and need large amounts of storage for tasks that do not require fast data access, HDDs are still a viable solution. On the other hand, for those who require high performance, reliability, and faster data access, SSDs are the superior choice. In many modern IT environments, a hybrid approach is often used, where both HDDs and SSDs are deployed together. This allows organizations to leverage the benefits of both technologies—using SSDs for high-performance tasks and HDDs for bulk storage.

Ultimately, the choice between HDDs and SSDs depends on a variety of factors, including performance requirements, budget, capacity needs, and reliability considerations. As technology continues to evolve, the capabilities of both types of drives will likely improve, and the cost difference between them will continue to narrow, making SSDs increasingly accessible for a wider range of applications. However, for now, both HDDs and SSDs have their place in modern storage architectures, and understanding their strengths and limitations is essential for building an efficient and effective storage solution.

Chapter 10: Storage Area Networks (SAN) and Network Attached Storage (NAS)

In modern IT environments, the management of data storage is one of the most critical aspects of infrastructure. As organizations handle increasingly large volumes of data, the need for robust, scalable, and reliable storage solutions has grown significantly. Two of the most commonly used storage technologies are Storage Area Networks (SAN) and Network Attached Storage (NAS). While both serve the primary purpose of providing storage resources to users and applications, they operate in fundamentally different ways. Understanding the differences between SAN and NAS, along with their respective advantages and use cases, is crucial for designing a storage architecture that meets the needs of an organization.

A Storage Area Network (SAN) is a dedicated, high-speed network that provides access to consolidated, block-level storage. Unlike traditional network storage solutions that operate at the file level, SAN operates at the block level, meaning that it treats storage devices as individual disks, making them available to servers just as if they were directly attached to those servers. SANs typically use protocols like Fibre Channel or iSCSI to connect servers to storage devices, providing fast and reliable data transfer rates. The primary advantage of a SAN is its ability to provide high-performance storage for applications that require fast access to large amounts of data. This makes SANs ideal for environments with heavy workloads, such as database servers, virtualized environments, and high-performance computing applications.

The architecture of a SAN is designed to be highly scalable and flexible. A SAN typically consists of multiple storage devices, such as disk arrays, connected to a network of servers. These devices can be located in different physical locations but are managed as a single unit, which simplifies storage administration. The centralized nature of a SAN allows for easier management of storage resources and the ability to allocate storage dynamically to various applications and users. Additionally, SANs provide redundancy and failover capabilities, ensuring that data remains available even in the event of a hardware failure. This makes SANs highly reliable and suitable for mission-critical applications where uptime is essential.

One of the key features of SANs is storage virtualization, which abstracts the physical storage hardware from the software applications that use it. This enables administrators to manage storage resources as a unified entity, regardless of the underlying hardware. With storage virtualization, administrators can easily allocate storage capacity, migrate data between devices, and optimize storage performance without disrupting applications or services. This capability is especially beneficial in environments that require frequent changes to storage configurations, such as data centers or cloud computing platforms. Additionally, SANs can be easily integrated into a broader disaster recovery strategy, as data can be replicated between geographically distributed SANs, providing protection against site-level failures.

Network Attached Storage (NAS), on the other hand, is a storage solution that provides file-level access to data over a network. Unlike SAN, which operates at the block level, NAS devices store data in files and share them across the network, allowing users and applications to access and manipulate the data using file protocols such as NFS (Network File System) or SMB (Server Message Block). NAS systems are typically used in environments where multiple users or systems need to access and share files, such as in file-sharing applications, backup systems, and collaborative workspaces. NAS is also highly effective for storing and managing unstructured data, such as documents, images, videos, and other types of content.

One of the primary advantages of NAS is its simplicity and ease of use. Unlike SANs, which require specialized knowledge and configuration, NAS systems are often plug-and-play devices that can be easily connected to a network and configured with minimal effort. They typically include a built-in operating system and user interface for managing storage, making them an ideal choice for small to medium-sized businesses that do not have dedicated IT staff. NAS systems are also cost-effective, offering a lower initial investment compared to SANs, which makes them accessible for organizations with limited budgets. Furthermore, NAS devices often include advanced features such as automated backups, data encryption, and access control, which help ensure the security and integrity of stored data.

NAS devices are highly scalable and can be expanded by adding additional drives or connecting multiple NAS units to create a larger, more distributed storage solution. However, while NAS offers ease of use and cost efficiency, it does have limitations when compared to SANs. Because NAS operates at the file level, it is generally slower than SAN in terms of data access speed. This makes NAS less suitable for high-performance applications that require low-latency access to large volumes of data, such as databases or virtual machines. Additionally, because NAS devices are connected via standard network protocols, the performance of the system can be affected by network congestion, which may limit throughput in environments with high data transfer demands.

Both SAN and NAS offer significant advantages, but their use cases differ based on the needs of the organization. SAN is typically used in environments that require high-performance, block-level access to storage, such as databases, virtualized infrastructures, and high-performance computing applications. It is well-suited for organizations that need to store large amounts of data and require fast, efficient access to that data across multiple servers. The block-level access provided by SAN allows for more granular control over storage, which can optimize performance and ensure that storage resources are allocated based on the specific needs of each application.

In contrast, NAS is often used for file-sharing applications, backup solutions, and other scenarios where multiple users or systems need to access and collaborate on data. NAS is an excellent solution for storing unstructured data and providing centralized access to files across a network. Its simplicity, cost-effectiveness, and ease of use make it an ideal choice for small to medium-sized businesses or for environments where fast data access is not as critical. NAS devices are also commonly used in home and small office environments for personal file storage, media streaming, and backups.

For organizations with more complex storage needs, it is not uncommon to see a combination of both SAN and NAS deployed within the same infrastructure. This hybrid approach allows businesses to take advantage of the high-performance capabilities of SAN while also leveraging the simplicity and cost-effectiveness of NAS for less performance-critical applications. By combining both technologies, organizations can optimize their storage solutions to meet the diverse needs of their users and applications.

As the demands for data storage continue to increase and technology evolves, the lines between SAN and NAS are becoming increasingly blurred. Newer technologies, such as Software-Defined Storage (SDS) and hybrid cloud storage, are being integrated into both SAN and NAS environments to provide greater flexibility, scalability, and cost efficiency. These technologies allow businesses to manage storage resources more dynamically, adapting to changing needs and leveraging both on-premises and cloud-based storage. The future of storage architecture will likely see continued advancements in both SAN and NAS technologies, with an increasing focus on integrating these solutions into larger, more flexible IT infrastructures. This evolution will provide organizations with even more powerful tools to manage their data, enhance performance, and improve scalability across a wide range of use cases.

Chapter 11: Storage Virtualization and Cloud Storage

In the rapidly evolving landscape of data storage, technologies like storage virtualization and cloud storage have transformed the way businesses manage their information. These technologies have introduced new levels of flexibility, scalability, and cost-efficiency, addressing the ever-growing need for organizations to store, access, and protect large volumes of data. Both storage virtualization and cloud storage offer unique advantages and, when combined, can significantly improve an organization's storage infrastructure by enabling more dynamic resource management, better disaster recovery options, and increased operational efficiency. Understanding how these technologies work, and how they interact with traditional storage systems, is key for organizations looking to optimize their data storage strategies.

Storage virtualization is a technology that abstracts the physical storage hardware from the software applications and users that access the data. This abstraction allows storage resources from multiple devices, whether they are hard disk drives, solid-state drives, or even networked storage arrays, to be pooled together and managed as a single, unified system. By virtualizing the storage infrastructure, administrators can allocate storage dynamically, distribute workloads more efficiently, and improve overall performance without being tied to specific physical storage devices. This level of flexibility not only improves resource utilization but also simplifies storage management, as administrators no longer have to worry about the specific details of individual storage devices. The virtualized environment provides a unified interface for managing storage, enabling more streamlined processes for provisioning, scaling, and maintaining data storage.

One of the key advantages of storage virtualization is its ability to simplify the management of storage resources. In traditional storage setups, administrators are required to manage each physical storage device individually, which can become increasingly complex as storage demands grow. With storage virtualization, administrators can manage storage resources as logical units, allowing them to allocate, resize, and migrate storage across physical devices with minimal disruption. This level of flexibility is especially valuable in environments where storage requirements frequently change or scale rapidly, such as in virtualized data centers or cloud-based infrastructures. Storage virtualization also enables organizations to consolidate their storage devices, reducing the number of physical devices needed and lowering the overall cost of managing and maintaining storage resources.

Moreover, storage virtualization offers significant benefits in terms of performance optimization. By pooling storage resources and optimizing their allocation, organizations can ensure that critical applications and services receive the necessary storage bandwidth. Virtualized storage systems can also implement techniques such as thin provisioning, where storage capacity is allocated on demand, reducing the need to over-provision storage and ensuring that resources are used efficiently. This results in cost savings, as businesses only pay for the storage they actually use, rather than reserving large amounts of storage that may never be fully utilized. Additionally, virtualized storage systems can implement data deduplication to eliminate redundant data, further optimizing storage capacity and improving performance.

Another significant benefit of storage virtualization is improved data protection and disaster recovery. In traditional storage setups, data is typically tied to specific physical devices, and recovering data in the event of a failure can be time-consuming and complex. With storage virtualization, data is abstracted from the physical hardware, which means that it can be more easily replicated, backed up, and restored. Virtualized storage systems can automate many of these processes, reducing the potential for human error and ensuring that critical data is protected. Virtualization also allows for live migration, which enables the movement of data and workloads between physical storage devices without downtime, enhancing the organization's ability to maintain high availability and reduce recovery times.

Cloud storage is another transformative technology that has become increasingly important in modern IT infrastructures. Unlike traditional on-premises storage systems, which require businesses to maintain their own physical storage devices and infrastructure, cloud storage provides a remote, off-site solution for storing data. Cloud storage is typically hosted by third-party providers, such as Amazon Web Services (AWS), Microsoft Azure, or Google Cloud, and offers organizations the ability to store data in data centers managed by the provider. This removes the need for businesses to invest in and manage their own storage infrastructure, allowing them to leverage the provider's resources and expertise. Cloud storage is available on-demand, meaning businesses can scale their storage capacity up or down as needed, without the need for large capital investments in hardware.

One of the primary advantages of cloud storage is scalability. With traditional storage systems, businesses need to predict their future storage needs and invest in infrastructure accordingly. This can result in over-provisioning, where businesses purchase more storage than they need, or under-provisioning, where they run out of capacity before they can scale. Cloud storage, on the other hand, provides virtually unlimited storage resources that can be scaled dynamically. This pay-as-you-go model allows organizations to only pay for the storage they actually use, which can result in significant cost savings. Cloud storage also offers flexibility, as data can be accessed from anywhere with an internet connection, making it an ideal solution for remote teams and businesses with multiple locations. This accessibility has become particularly important in today's world, where businesses need to be agile and responsive to changing conditions.

Cloud storage also improves data redundancy and disaster recovery. Most cloud providers store data across multiple data centers in different geographical regions, ensuring that data is replicated and protected in the event of a site failure or disaster. This distributed approach minimizes the risk of data loss and ensures that businesses can quickly recover their data if needed. Additionally, many cloud providers offer automatic backups and versioning, allowing businesses to easily roll back to previous versions of files in the event of accidental deletion or corruption. Cloud storage providers typically have strong security protocols in place, including encryption and access controls, to ensure that data remains safe from unauthorized access.

Despite its many advantages, cloud storage also comes with some challenges. One of the primary concerns is security, particularly in industries that handle sensitive data, such as healthcare or finance. Storing data off-site introduces the risk that it could be accessed by unauthorized parties, and businesses must carefully evaluate the security measures in place to protect their data. Compliance with data protection regulations, such as the General Data Protection Regulation (GDPR) or the Health Insurance Portability and Accountability Act (HIPAA), is also a key consideration for organizations using cloud storage. Additionally, businesses must consider the bandwidth required to upload and download large amounts of data, as high transfer costs can add up over time.

The integration of storage virtualization and cloud storage has further transformed how organizations manage their data. Many cloud storage providers now offer virtualization capabilities, allowing businesses to manage and scale their storage resources more dynamically. With cloud-based storage virtualization, organizations can combine the benefits of virtualization, such as automated provisioning and resource optimization, with the flexibility and scalability of the cloud. This integration creates a more agile storage infrastructure that can quickly adapt to changing business needs.

As organizations continue to face growing data storage demands, both storage virtualization and cloud storage will play increasingly important roles in modern IT environments. These technologies offer a powerful combination of flexibility, scalability, performance, and cost-efficiency, making them essential components of any modern data storage strategy. By understanding how these technologies work and how they complement each other, organizations can build storage infrastructures that are optimized for today's fast-paced, data-driven world.

Chapter 12: RAID (Redundant Array of Independent Disks) Configurations

RAID, or Redundant Array of Independent Disks, is a technology that is widely used in server environments to improve storage performance, provide data redundancy, and increase the overall reliability of storage systems. The concept of RAID is based on the idea of combining multiple physical hard drives into a single logical unit to achieve various benefits, including better performance, data protection, and scalability. There are several different RAID configurations, each offering distinct advantages depending on the specific needs of an organization. Understanding how these configurations work and what they offer can help businesses make informed decisions about how to structure their storage systems for optimal performance and security.

At its core, RAID is designed to address two critical issues in traditional storage setups: data redundancy and storage performance. Data redundancy ensures that if one disk fails, the data stored on that disk is not lost. Performance improvements come from distributing data across multiple disks in a way that allows for faster read and write operations. RAID configurations use different techniques to achieve these objectives, and the configuration chosen will depend on the particular requirements of the environment, including the need for speed, fault tolerance, and storage capacity.

One of the most basic RAID configurations is RAID 0, also known as striping. In this setup, data is split into blocks and distributed evenly across multiple drives. By spreading the data across multiple disks, RAID 0 improves read and write speeds because the system can read or write to several disks simultaneously. This makes RAID 0 an excellent choice for applications that require high-speed data access, such as video editing, gaming, and high-performance computing tasks. However, RAID 0 provides no redundancy. If one drive fails, all data is lost because there is no backup of the data on other drives. While RAID 0 offers improved performance, it is best suited for environments where speed is more important than data security.

In contrast, RAID 1, also known as mirroring, provides data redundancy by duplicating the same data across two or more drives. In this configuration, all data is written identically to each drive in the array. The primary benefit of RAID 1 is its fault tolerance: if one drive fails, the data remains accessible from the other drive(s). However, the trade-off for this redundancy is that storage capacity is halved, as each drive contains an exact copy of the data. RAID 1 is often used in environments where data integrity and uptime are critical, such as in file servers, email servers, and systems that handle sensitive information. While RAID 1 ensures high availability and data protection, it is not as efficient in terms of storage utilization as some other RAID levels.

RAID 5 is one of the most commonly used configurations in enterprise environments, combining both striping and parity for improved performance and redundancy. In a RAID 5 setup, data is striped across multiple drives (like in RAID 0), but it also includes a parity block that is distributed across all drives in the array. Parity is a form of error-checking that allows the system to rebuild data if a drive fails. The parity information is calculated based on the data stored on the other drives, allowing the lost data to be reconstructed. RAID 5 offers a good balance of performance, redundancy, and storage efficiency. While RAID 5 can tolerate the failure of one drive without data loss, the system will experience degraded performance during the rebuild process. RAID 5 requires a minimum of three drives and is widely used in environments where a combination of performance and fault tolerance is needed, such as in database servers and file storage systems.

A variation of RAID 5 is RAID 6, which improves on RAID 5 by adding an additional parity block, thus providing more redundancy. In a RAID 6 setup, data is striped across multiple drives, and two sets of parity data are stored across the array. This allows RAID 6 to tolerate the failure of two drives simultaneously, which makes it more fault-tolerant than RAID 5. However, this added redundancy comes at the cost of write performance, as two sets of parity information need to be calculated and written during every write operation. RAID 6 is ideal for environments that require high levels of data protection and can tolerate the additional performance overhead, such as in mission-critical applications, archival storage, or large-scale data centers.

For organizations that require high performance without a heavy focus on redundancy, RAID 10 (also known as RAID 1+0) is a popular choice. RAID 10 is a combination of RAID 1 (mirroring) and RAID 0 (striping). In this configuration, data is mirrored across pairs of drives, and then these mirrors are striped across multiple pairs of drives. RAID 10 provides the fault tolerance of RAID 1, while also offering the performance benefits of RAID 0. This configuration requires at least four drives and offers a good balance between performance and redundancy. However, as with RAID 1, the storage capacity is reduced by half, as each piece of data is stored on multiple drives. RAID 10 is particularly well-suited for applications that require both high-speed data access and fault tolerance, such as in transactional databases or high-performance server environments.

In addition to these common RAID configurations, there are also several other variations designed for specific use cases. RAID 50 is a combination of RAID 5 and RAID 0, offering the performance benefits of RAID 0 while providing the redundancy of RAID 5. It is typically used in environments that require a higher level of performance than standard RAID 5 but still need the ability to recover data in case of a drive failure. Similarly, RAID 60 is a combination of RAID 6 and RAID 0, offering the redundancy of RAID 6 with the performance improvements of RAID 0.

While RAID configurations can significantly improve the performance and reliability of storage systems, it is important to note that they are not a substitute for backup. RAID provides redundancy within a specific array, but it does not protect against data loss due to accidental deletion, corruption, or catastrophic events like fire or flood. Therefore, RAID should be used in conjunction with a comprehensive backup strategy to ensure that data is fully protected.

The choice of RAID configuration depends largely on the specific needs of the organization. RAID 0 is ideal for environments where speed is the highest priority, and data loss is less of a concern. RAID 1 is suitable for applications where data protection and uptime are critical, but the cost of additional storage is acceptable. RAID 5 and RAID 6 strike a balance between performance and redundancy, while RAID 10 offers high performance with strong fault tolerance. Ultimately, understanding the strengths and limitations of each RAID level is key to selecting the right solution for the specific storage requirements of any organization.

Chapter 14: Server Power Management and Redundancy

Power management and redundancy are crucial aspects of server infrastructure, ensuring that systems remain operational, efficient, and resilient under all conditions. As businesses increasingly rely on technology for critical operations, the demand for uninterrupted service and the minimization of downtime has never been greater. Power management involves not only ensuring that servers receive the necessary electrical supply but also optimizing energy consumption, minimizing waste, and extending the lifespan of the hardware. Redundancy, on the other hand, refers to the inclusion of backup systems to ensure that, in the event of a failure, the server continues to function without disruption. These two elements work hand-in-hand to support the continuous, reliable performance of a server environment, which is particularly important in data centers, cloud computing environments, and enterprise applications.

Effective server power management is about more than just providing a stable power supply; it is about optimizing energy use to balance performance with energy consumption. Servers, particularly in large data centers, consume a significant amount of power. The challenge lies in managing this power usage to avoid unnecessary energy expenditure while maintaining the required performance. To achieve this, modern servers are equipped with advanced power management features that allow them to adjust power usage based on demand. These features can automatically adjust the server's power consumption depending on its workload, reducing power use during low-activity periods and ramping up only when higher processing power is needed. For instance, processors in modern servers can adjust their power states, switching to lower power modes when the full capacity of the CPU is not needed.

Moreover, server manufacturers often design power supplies with high efficiency in mind. Efficient power supplies convert more of the incoming electricity into usable power, reducing waste heat and improving overall energy efficiency. These power supplies are typically rated according to standards such as 80 PLUS certification, which ensures that the power supply delivers at least 80% efficiency across a range of loads. By using efficient power supplies, data centers and businesses can significantly reduce their overall energy consumption, which not only helps with cost savings but also contributes to environmental sustainability by reducing carbon footprints.

Power management also involves the monitoring and control of power usage across the server infrastructure. Intelligent power distribution units (PDUs) are often used to manage the power delivered to each server. These devices can be monitored remotely, allowing administrators to track power consumption patterns, identify inefficiencies, and even control power supply to individual servers or racks. This level of control provides administrators with the ability to optimize power usage further, identify equipment that is consuming more power than necessary, and take action to reduce energy costs. For example, if a server is operating at less than optimal capacity and drawing excessive power, it can be shut down or replaced with more efficient hardware.

In addition to power management, redundancy plays an equally important role in ensuring the reliability and availability of server infrastructure. Redundancy refers to the inclusion of backup systems that ensure continuous operation in the event of a failure in the primary system. For example, in the context of power, redundancy is provided through uninterruptible power supplies (UPS) and redundant power supplies (RPS). A UPS is a critical device in any server environment, providing backup power when the main power supply fails. In the event of a power outage, the UPS ensures that the servers remain operational for a brief period, allowing administrators to either switch to a backup power source or shut down the systems in an orderly manner to prevent data loss or hardware damage.

Redundant power supplies, which are often found in enterprise-level servers, further enhance reliability by providing multiple power sources to the server. In these configurations, if one power supply fails, the other can take over without any disruption in service. This eliminates a single point of failure and ensures that the server remains powered even in the case of a hardware malfunction. Redundant power supplies are particularly important in mission-critical environments where even a brief interruption in power can lead to significant disruptions in business operations.

Beyond power, data and hardware redundancy are also integral to maintaining server uptime and preventing data loss. Hardware redundancy ensures that the failure of individual components does not impact the overall system. This can include redundant hard drives, network connections, and even server components like processors and memory. For example, in a server setup using RAID (Redundant Array of Independent Disks) technology, data is distributed across multiple drives, allowing for continued access to the data even if one or more drives fail. RAID configurations such as RAID 1 (mirroring) or RAID 5 (striping with parity) provide the necessary redundancy to protect data without significantly affecting performance.

In addition to hardware, network redundancy is essential in modern server environments. Servers rely heavily on network connections for communication with other servers, clients, and cloud services. Redundant network connections ensure that if one network link fails, another can take over without disrupting service. This is particularly important in environments where high availability is critical, such as in online services, financial institutions, or e-commerce platforms. Redundant network paths, such as dual Ethernet cables or fiber optic connections, provide resilience in the face of potential network outages.

For mission-critical applications, geographical redundancy is another important consideration. Geographical redundancy involves duplicating server infrastructure across different physical locations. In the event of a disaster or localized outage—such as a power failure, natural disaster, or fire—the backup site can take over the operations of the primary site. This is commonly seen in cloud computing, where data centers are distributed across multiple regions to ensure high availability and data protection. Cloud service providers often incorporate geographical redundancy as part of their service offerings to guarantee service continuity for their customers.

Server redundancy extends to the software layer as well. Virtualization plays a crucial role in redundancy by allowing workloads to be moved seamlessly from one server to another. In the event of a server failure, virtual machines (VMs) can be migrated to another host in a matter of seconds or minutes, minimizing downtime and maintaining business continuity. Additionally, redundancy in software configurations, such as failover clustering and load balancing, ensures that if one server or application instance fails, another can immediately handle the workload, maintaining service levels without interruption.

Managing power and redundancy effectively requires a holistic approach that encompasses hardware, software, and operational processes. By carefully designing server infrastructure with power efficiency and redundancy in mind, businesses can ensure the reliability, availability, and scalability of their systems. A failure in power or hardware can have significant consequences for business operations, and addressing these issues through thoughtful power management and redundancy is critical to maintaining uninterrupted service. As organizations continue to scale their IT environments and embrace new technologies like cloud computing, the need for effective power management and redundancy will only grow, making these aspects of server infrastructure even more important in the years to come.

Chapter 15: Cooling Systems and Server Room Management

The proper management of a server room is a critical aspect of ensuring the longevity, reliability, and performance of an organization's IT infrastructure. Among the most important considerations in server room management is the cooling system, which plays a crucial role in maintaining the optimal operating conditions for servers and other hardware. Servers and data center equipment generate a significant amount of heat during operation, and without an effective cooling system, the temperature inside the server room can rise to levels that may damage the hardware, reduce performance, and ultimately lead to failures or system downtime. Therefore, understanding the different types of cooling systems, how they function, and how to manage the server room environment is essential for IT professionals responsible for the upkeep of such facilities.

Servers generate heat as they process data, run applications, and perform other tasks. The hardware components within servers, particularly the central processing units (CPUs), graphics processing units (GPUs), and storage devices, are susceptible to overheating, which can cause thermal throttling, system crashes, or permanent hardware damage. As the density of servers in data centers and server rooms increases, so does the amount of heat generated. This creates the need for sophisticated cooling solutions to prevent thermal-related issues that could impair system reliability. A properly designed cooling system not only mitigates these risks but also ensures that servers run at peak performance levels, extending the lifespan of the hardware and preventing unexpected downtime.

The most common cooling systems used in server rooms and data centers are air cooling and liquid cooling. Air cooling is the traditional method used in most server rooms, relying on the movement of cool air across server components to dissipate heat. This method typically involves the use of fans, air conditioning units, and ventilation systems to circulate cold air through the room and expel hot air. Air cooling systems are relatively simple to implement and maintain, making them an economical choice for many businesses. The cooling process works by drawing cooler air from outside the server room or data center and circulating it through racks of servers, where the heat is absorbed. The warm air is then removed by exhaust fans or HVAC systems, which maintain a steady flow of air to regulate temperature levels.

In a server room, air cooling can be enhanced with the use of hot aisle/cold aisle containment. This layout involves arranging the server racks in alternating rows, where the front of the racks faces cold air and the back of the racks faces hot air. Cold air is drawn into the servers from the cold aisle, and after the servers dissipate heat, the warm air is expelled into the hot aisle. This separation helps to prevent hot and cold air from mixing, improving the overall efficiency of the cooling system. Another technique used to optimize air cooling is rack-mounted fans or server fans, which are designed to increase airflow around individual servers, helping to cool them more effectively.

While air cooling is widely used, liquid cooling has emerged as a more efficient and effective solution for managing heat in high-density server environments. Liquid cooling uses the principle of heat exchange, transferring heat from the server components to a liquid coolant, which is then circulated through pipes or heat exchangers to dissipate the heat. This method is particularly useful in environments where air cooling would not be sufficient due to the sheer density of the equipment or the high performance requirements of the systems. Direct-to-chip liquid cooling is one example, where liquid coolant is routed directly to the components that generate the most heat, such as the CPU or GPU. This targeted cooling approach minimizes the overall heat buildup in the system and can achieve much lower temperatures compared to traditional air cooling.

One of the key advantages of liquid cooling is its ability to transfer heat more efficiently. Liquid has a higher thermal conductivity than air, meaning it can carry away heat more effectively, reducing the need for large fans and air conditioners. This makes liquid cooling a highly efficient solution for high-performance computing environments, such as those used in artificial intelligence (AI), machine learning (ML), and scientific simulations, where servers generate large amounts of heat. Additionally, liquid cooling can reduce the overall energy consumption of a server room, as it can achieve better cooling with less energy expenditure compared to air-based systems.

While cooling systems are essential for server room management, the overall environment within the server room also needs to be carefully monitored and controlled. Temperature and humidity are two critical factors that affect the performance and longevity of servers. Servers typically operate best in a temperature range of 18 to 27 degrees Celsius (64 to 80 degrees Fahrenheit). Any deviation from this range can result in performance degradation or, in extreme cases, hardware failure. Excessive heat can cause components to overheat, while cold temperatures can lead to condensation, which may damage electrical components. Similarly, humidity levels should be controlled to prevent moisture buildup, which can cause corrosion and short-circuiting of server components. Humidity levels in a server room should generally be kept between 45% and 60% to avoid such issues.

To ensure that the server room is maintained within these optimal conditions, temperature and humidity sensors are often installed throughout the room. These sensors are connected to monitoring systems that provide real-time data, allowing IT personnel to detect any fluctuations in temperature or humidity levels and take corrective actions before the situation becomes critical. Automated alerts can notify staff of potential issues, allowing for rapid response times and reducing the risk of equipment damage or downtime.

Another important aspect of server room management is airflow management. Proper airflow is necessary to ensure that cool air reaches all components that require cooling, while warm air is efficiently expelled from the room. A poorly designed airflow system can result in hot spots, where the temperature exceeds safe operating levels. This can lead to overheating of components, increased fan noise, and reduced performance. By using techniques like cold aisle and hot aisle containment, as well as airflow optimization tools such as blanking panels and vented tiles, server rooms can achieve better airflow efficiency. These tools help to prevent cold air from escaping into unwanted areas and direct it toward the servers that need it most.

Server room management also involves regular maintenance to ensure that the cooling systems remain operational and efficient. Dust, dirt, and debris can accumulate on fans, air filters, and vents, reducing airflow and hindering the cooling process. Therefore, it is essential to schedule routine cleaning and inspections of the cooling systems and equipment. Additionally, air conditioning units, fans, and liquid cooling systems must be monitored and maintained to ensure that they are operating at peak efficiency. Failure to maintain these systems can lead to system failures, overheating, and downtime, which can have serious consequences for business operations.

The management of power and cooling in a server room is an ongoing process that requires constant monitoring and optimization. As server environments continue to grow and become more complex, the need for advanced cooling systems and effective management practices will only increase. Whether using air cooling or liquid cooling systems, proper temperature regulation, humidity control, and airflow management are essential for maintaining the stability and performance of a server room. As technologies evolve, the integration of cooling systems and server room management practices will continue to play a pivotal role in supporting the ever-expanding demands of modern IT infrastructure.

Chapter 16: Server Deployment and Configuration

Deploying and configuring servers is a critical task in the IT infrastructure process that requires careful planning, execution, and ongoing management to ensure that servers operate efficiently, securely, and reliably. Whether the deployment involves a single server or an entire server farm, the process includes a series of steps to install, configure, and optimize hardware and software so that the server can fulfill its intended role within the network. This chapter delves into the various stages of server deployment and configuration, highlighting key factors and considerations that IT professionals must address to ensure the success of the deployment.

The first stage in the server deployment process is planning. This stage is crucial because it sets the foundation for everything that follows. Before deploying a server, organizations must clearly define the role the server will play within the network. Whether it will act as a web server, database server, file server, or something else, understanding the server's purpose allows IT teams to determine the necessary hardware specifications, software requirements, and network configurations. This phase also involves ensuring that there is adequate power, cooling, and space within the server room or data center, as these physical elements are just as important as the software components in maintaining server performance and reliability.

Once the planning phase is complete, the next step is the installation of the server hardware and software. The server hardware must be properly set up, which includes physically mounting the server in a rack (if applicable), connecting power supplies, network cables, and other peripherals, and ensuring that the system is ready for operation. For most businesses, this involves installing a server operating system (OS), which is the foundation for all other software and services that will run on the server. The choice of OS, whether it is Windows Server, Linux, or a specialized operating system, depends largely on the intended use of the server and the existing IT infrastructure. The installation process may involve configuring system settings such as disk partitions, file systems, and basic network settings, such as static IP addresses.

During the configuration stage, IT administrators begin to fine-tune the server to meet the specific requirements of the organization. This step involves configuring the network settings to ensure that the server is properly integrated into the existing network architecture. Depending on the server's role, this might include setting up DNS, DHCP, and active directory services, or configuring access controls for remote administration. In addition to networking, administrators will typically configure various hardware components, including RAID arrays for storage, setting up backup solutions, and ensuring that firewall and security configurations are in place to protect the server from potential threats.

Security is a central aspect of server configuration. Servers often house sensitive information and services, which makes them a target for cyberattacks. As part of the configuration process, IT professionals must ensure that the server is properly secured. This includes configuring user accounts, setting up permissions for file access, and enabling encryption where necessary. Additionally, it is essential to implement security patches and updates to protect the server from vulnerabilities. Many organizations adopt a security policy that defines how often updates are applied and how security patches are tested before they are rolled out across the infrastructure. Implementing strong security configurations, such as configuring multi-factor authentication (MFA) or limiting access to specific IP addresses, adds another layer of protection for the server.

Another key part of the configuration phase is ensuring that the server has the necessary software installed and configured to perform its intended tasks. For example, a web server might require the installation of web server software, such as Apache or Nginx, while a database server will need the appropriate database management system, like MySQL or Microsoft SQL Server. Administrators will also install any additional software or services that the server needs to run its applications, such as monitoring tools, antivirus programs, or logging services. It is also essential to configure these programs properly, including establishing parameters like resource allocation and load balancing settings, to ensure that the server operates at peak performance.

After the hardware and software configuration is complete, the server needs to undergo thorough testing. Testing helps verify that all configurations have been implemented correctly and that the server performs as expected under different conditions. This step involves stress testing the system to ensure that it can handle high traffic or workloads, checking network connectivity to ensure proper communication between servers and other network devices, and verifying the performance of all installed software. Additionally, security testing is vital to ensure that the server is resistant to attacks. Penetration testing and other forms of vulnerability scanning help identify potential weaknesses in the server's security configuration, which can then be mitigated before the server goes live.

Once testing has been completed successfully, the server is ready for deployment into the live environment. This involves connecting the server to the network and making it available for users and applications. Depending on the type of server, this may also involve configuring load balancing and ensuring that the server can scale to handle increased demands. For example, a web server might be part of a clustered system that includes multiple servers to distribute the load of handling web traffic. In such cases, configuring load balancing software ensures that each server in the cluster receives a proportionate amount of traffic and that resources are used efficiently.

Monitoring and maintenance are ongoing parts of server deployment. Once the server is live, it must be monitored continuously to ensure that it is operating correctly. Server monitoring tools track metrics such as CPU usage, memory consumption, disk space, and network traffic, providing administrators with real-time data on the server's performance. Additionally, monitoring the server's security status is crucial to ensure that unauthorized access or potential vulnerabilities are quickly detected and addressed. Maintenance tasks include applying regular software updates, security patches, and ensuring that backups are performed on a scheduled basis to protect against data loss. The ongoing monitoring and maintenance of servers help prevent issues before they arise and ensure that the server remains operational and secure.

As the demands of modern IT environments grow, server deployment and configuration will continue to evolve. New technologies and automation tools, such as containerization and orchestration platforms, are reshaping how servers are deployed and managed. These tools allow IT teams to automate many aspects of server configuration, deployment, and scaling, improving efficiency and reducing human error. For example, Docker and Kubernetes are widely used for deploying containerized applications, offering a more flexible and scalable way to manage server resources in cloud environments.

Server deployment and configuration is a detailed and structured process that requires careful planning, execution, and ongoing management. From the installation of hardware to the configuration of software, network settings, and security protocols, every step plays a crucial role in ensuring that the server performs optimally and securely. Whether setting up a single server or an entire server farm, understanding the importance of each stage in the deployment process allows IT professionals to deliver a high-performing, reliable, and secure server environment that meets the needs of the organization.

Chapter 17: Network Basics for IT Infrastructure

In today's digital world, networking forms the backbone of every IT infrastructure. From simple home networks to complex data centers, networks enable devices to communicate with each other, share resources, and access critical information. A strong understanding of network fundamentals is essential for anyone involved in designing, deploying, or managing IT infrastructure. This chapter will explore the basics of networking, providing insights into the various components that make up a network, how they function, and their role in supporting the overall IT environment.

At the most fundamental level, a network is simply a collection of devices that are connected together to enable communication. These devices can range from computers, printers, and servers to mobile devices, routers, and switches. The purpose of a network is to facilitate the exchange of data and resources between these devices. Whether it's sharing files, accessing the internet, or sending emails, networking provides the necessary infrastructure for digital communication. The two most common types of networks are Local Area Networks (LANs) and Wide Area Networks (WANs). A LAN typically spans a small geographic area, such as an office or a building, and is used to connect devices within that area. A WAN, on the other hand, connects devices across a larger geographic area, such as multiple office locations or even global networks. The internet itself is a vast example of a WAN, connecting millions of devices worldwide.

To enable communication between devices, networks rely on network protocols, which are standardized rules that govern how data is transmitted across a network. The most widely used protocol is Transmission Control Protocol/Internet Protocol (TCP/IP). This suite of protocols is the foundation of modern networking and enables devices to communicate over the internet and local networks. TCP/IP is composed of several layers, each responsible for different aspects of data transmission. The IP layer is responsible for addressing and routing data packets, while the TCP layer ensures that data is delivered accurately and in the correct order. The combination of these protocols allows devices to send and receive data efficiently and reliably.

In addition to protocols, network hardware plays a crucial role in the functionality of a network. Key network devices include routers, switches, modems, and hubs, each serving a distinct purpose. A router is responsible for directing data packets between different networks, such as between a local network and the internet. Routers use IP addresses to determine the best path for data to travel and ensure that data reaches its intended destination. A switch, on the other hand, operates within a single network, connecting devices like computers and servers. Switches help manage data traffic within the network by forwarding data packets to the correct device based on its MAC address. A hub is a simpler device that also connects multiple devices within a network but does so by broadcasting data to all connected devices, making it less efficient than a switch. A modem is used to connect a local network to the internet, converting digital data from the network into analog signals that can travel over telephone lines or cable systems.

Understanding the concept of IP addressing is crucial for network configuration. Each device on a network needs a unique identifier to ensure that data can be accurately routed to it. This identifier is called an IP address. An IP address is a numerical label assigned to each device on a network. The most commonly used version of IP addressing is IPv4, which uses a 32-bit address space, allowing for approximately 4.3 billion unique addresses. However, with the growth of the internet and the increasing number of devices, IPv6 was introduced, using a 128-bit address space and providing a virtually unlimited number of addresses. IP addresses are typically assigned dynamically by a Dynamic Host Configuration Protocol (DHCP) server, which automatically assigns addresses to devices as they connect to the network. In some cases, static IP addresses may be assigned manually to devices that require a fixed address, such as servers or network printers.

Once devices are connected to the network, the flow of data must be carefully managed to ensure optimal performance and reliability. One important consideration is bandwidth, which refers to the amount of data that can be transmitted over a network in a given period of time. Bandwidth is typically measured in bits per second (bps), with higher values indicating faster data transfer speeds. Bandwidth is a key factor in determining how well a network can handle multiple users or large volumes of data. However, it's important to note that high bandwidth alone does not guarantee good network performance. Network latency, which refers to the delay in transmitting data across a network, is also an important factor. High latency can cause delays in communication, especially in real-time applications like video conferencing or online gaming. Latency can be influenced by various factors, including the physical distance between devices, the quality of the network infrastructure, and network congestion.

Another important concept in networking is network security. As networks become more complex and interconnected, ensuring their security becomes increasingly important. Security threats, such as unauthorized access, malware, and denial-of-service attacks, can disrupt network operations and compromise sensitive data. To protect networks, organizations implement a variety of security measures, including firewalls, intrusion detection systems (IDS), and encryption. A firewall acts as a barrier between a trusted internal network and an untrusted external network (such as the internet), filtering traffic based on predefined security rules. An IDS monitors network traffic for signs of malicious activity, alerting administrators to potential security breaches. Encryption is used to secure data transmitted over a network, making it unreadable to unauthorized users.

As businesses and organizations expand their IT infrastructure, networks often need to be scalable to accommodate growing demands. Scalability refers to the ability of a network to handle an increasing number of devices, users, and data traffic without a significant decline in performance. To achieve scalability, organizations often use network segmentation, dividing the network into smaller sub-networks, or VLANs (Virtual Local Area Networks). This allows for more efficient use of bandwidth and improves security by isolating traffic within different segments. Additionally, load balancing techniques can be employed to distribute network traffic evenly across multiple servers or network paths, ensuring that no single resource is overwhelmed.

In addition to physical networking, cloud-based networking is becoming increasingly popular as organizations shift towards cloud computing. Cloud networking enables businesses to connect their on-premises network to cloud services, allowing for seamless access to cloud-based resources and applications. Cloud service providers like Amazon Web Services (AWS), Microsoft Azure, and Google Cloud offer various networking solutions, such as virtual private networks (VPNs) and dedicated connections, to help organizations securely integrate their on-premises infrastructure with the cloud.

Network management is a critical task in maintaining the overall health and performance of an IT infrastructure. Network administrators use a variety of network management tools to monitor, configure, and troubleshoot the network. These tools provide real-time insights into network traffic, device status, and performance metrics, allowing administrators to quickly identify and address issues. Effective network management ensures that the network operates efficiently, securely, and without interruption, supporting the broader goals of the organization.

Understanding network basics is essential for anyone involved in IT infrastructure. Networks form the foundation for communication, data transfer, and the delivery of critical services across organizations. By understanding the components that make up a network, how data flows through it, and the factors that influence its performance and security, IT professionals can design, deploy, and manage robust network systems that meet the growing demands of modern business environments.

Chapter 18: Ethernet and Networking Standards

Ethernet has become the backbone of most local area networks (LANs) and is one of the most widely used networking technologies in both residential and enterprise environments. Initially developed in the 1970s, Ethernet has undergone significant evolution over the decades, enabling faster speeds, improved reliability, and greater scalability. The development of networking standards has played a crucial role in the evolution of Ethernet, ensuring interoperability between different devices and systems, and enabling global communication. This chapter will explore the history of Ethernet, the key networking standards associated with it, and how these standards have contributed to the modern networking landscape.

At its core, Ethernet is a protocol used for connecting devices in a LAN, enabling them to communicate with one another. The original Ethernet standard, defined by Xerox Corporation in collaboration with DEC and Intel, used coaxial cables to transmit data at speeds of 10 megabits per second (Mbps). Over time, Ethernet evolved to use twisted-pair cables and fiber-optic cables, and its speeds have increased dramatically, reaching up to 400 gigabits per second (Gbps) in modern applications. The continued development of Ethernet standards has allowed it to remain relevant as networking demands have grown, especially with the rise of high-speed internet, cloud computing, and data-intensive applications.

One of the most significant factors contributing to the widespread adoption of Ethernet is the open standard nature of the protocol. Unlike proprietary networking technologies that were locked to specific vendors or hardware, Ethernet standards were developed and published by organizations such as the Institute of Electrical and Electronics Engineers (IEEE) and International Organization for Standardization (ISO). This openness allowed multiple manufacturers to build Ethernet-compatible devices, creating a competitive market and driving down costs. This, in turn, made Ethernet a cost-effective and scalable solution for networking.

The IEEE 802 family of standards has been essential in the evolution of Ethernet. The IEEE 802.3 standard specifically defines the specifications for Ethernet networking, covering both wired and wireless communication. This standard includes a wide variety of media types, including twisted-pair copper cables, fiber optics, and coaxial cables, each of which is designed to meet different networking needs. The standard has undergone numerous revisions to improve performance, support higher speeds, and introduce new features such as full-duplex communication, which allows for simultaneous sending and receiving of data.

The Ethernet frame is the basic unit of data transmission in an Ethernet network. It consists of several components, including the destination address, source address, payload (the actual data being transmitted), and a checksum for error detection. This frame structure ensures that data is transmitted efficiently and accurately across the network. Ethernet frames are typically transmitted using broadcasting or multicasting, where a single frame is sent to multiple devices, allowing for efficient communication in a network with many nodes.

Ethernet has evolved to support increasingly faster speeds, with new standards emerging to accommodate higher data transmission needs. The first major milestone was the introduction of Fast Ethernet (100BASE-TX), which increased the speed to 100 Mbps. The development of Gigabit Ethernet (1000BASE-T) followed, offering speeds of 1 gigabit per second (Gbps). As networking demands continued to grow, 10 Gigabit Ethernet (10GbE) was introduced, supporting speeds of 10 Gbps, and newer standards such as 40 Gigabit Ethernet and 100 Gigabit Ethernet were introduced to address the needs of large data centers, high-performance computing, and enterprise-level networks. These high-speed standards rely on fiber-optic cables, which offer much higher bandwidth than traditional copper cables, and are designed to support long-distance communication across data centers and between cities.

Ethernet's adaptability has extended beyond wired networks to include wireless applications as well. While Ethernet traditionally referred to wired LAN connections, modern Ethernet standards have extended to wireless communication technologies through the development of Wi-Fi standards, which are often based on Ethernet principles. Wi-Fi allows devices to connect to a network without physical cables, providing flexibility and mobility within organizations. Wi-Fi technologies are governed by the IEEE 802.11 standard, which, while separate from the Ethernet standards, complements Ethernet in many networking environments.

The impact of Ethernet's evolution is most apparent in its ability to scale. Initially used for relatively simple networking environments, Ethernet today serves as the backbone of global communication systems, including the internet, data centers, and private enterprise networks. The ability to scale Ethernet from small office LANs to large, complex networks has made it an indispensable tool in modern IT infrastructure. As the demand for faster data speeds and greater bandwidth continues to grow, Ethernet's ability to adapt to these needs will ensure its continued dominance in networking.

Alongside Ethernet, networking standards such as IP (Internet Protocol) and TCP/IP (Transmission Control Protocol/Internet Protocol) are critical to the overall functioning of modern networks. IP addresses are used to identify devices on a network, while TCP/IP ensures that data is transmitted reliably and in the correct order. These protocols work in tandem with Ethernet to enable devices to communicate over a wide variety of network types, from local area networks to the global internet. The combination of Ethernet's physical network infrastructure and the IP/TCP stack creates the foundation for modern networking, allowing businesses and individuals to share data and access resources across the world.

Network security has also evolved alongside Ethernet to protect against a growing array of threats. As Ethernet networks have become larger and more complex, the need for robust security measures has intensified. Standards such as 802.1X provide mechanisms for authenticating devices and users before they can access the network, ensuring that only authorized users are allowed entry. Encryption protocols, such as IPsec, help secure data as it travels over Ethernet networks, protecting it from interception and unauthorized access. Furthermore, network monitoring and intrusion detection systems are vital for identifying and responding to potential security threats within an Ethernet network.

Ethernet continues to evolve to meet the demands of modern IT infrastructure. The introduction of 100G Ethernet and 400G Ethernet represents the next frontier in networking speeds, offering greater capacity and faster data transfer rates for high-bandwidth applications. These new Ethernet standards are designed to support data-heavy applications such as video streaming, cloud computing, and the growing use of big data analytics.

Ethernet's flexibility and scalability are key reasons why it has remained the dominant networking standard for decades. It has seamlessly adapted to the changing needs of businesses, data centers, and service providers, providing high-speed connectivity, reliability, and a robust framework for global communication. The continued development of Ethernet standards ensures that the technology will remain central to networking for the foreseeable future, supporting an ever-growing range of applications and services that are shaping the digital landscape.

Chapter 19: IP Addressing and Subnetting in Networking

IP addressing and subnetting are foundational concepts in networking, forming the basis for communication across different devices and networks. These concepts are integral to the design, organization, and management of modern networks, whether in a local area network (LAN), a wide area network (WAN), or the global internet itself. IP addresses are the unique identifiers assigned to devices within a network, allowing them to communicate and exchange data. Subnetting, on the other hand, is the process of dividing a large network into smaller, more manageable subnetworks, which helps improve performance, security, and scalability.

The IP address is a numerical label used to identify a device on a network. It ensures that data can be routed correctly from one device to another across the internet or within a local network. An IP address is typically represented as a series of four octets, with each octet being a number between 0 and 255, separated by periods (e.g., 192.168.1.1). This format is known as IPv4 (Internet Protocol version 4), which uses a 32-bit addressing scheme. IPv4 can support approximately 4.3 billion unique addresses, which, although a vast number, has proven to be insufficient in the face of the explosive growth of internet-connected devices. As a result, IPv6 (Internet Protocol version 6) was developed, using a 128-bit addressing scheme and vastly expanding the address space to accommodate the ever-growing number of devices connected to the internet.

IP addresses can be divided into two categories: public and private. A public IP address is a unique address assigned to a device that is directly accessible from the internet. These addresses are assigned by the Internet Assigned Numbers Authority (IANA) and are used to route traffic across the internet. On the other hand, private IP addresses are used within private networks and are not directly accessible from the internet. These addresses are part of specific IP address ranges set aside for private use by the IANA. Devices within a private network can communicate with each other using private IP addresses, but they need a network address translation (NAT) device, such as a router, to access the internet.

The use of private IP addresses is particularly important in large-scale networks, where multiple devices need to be connected internally without using up the limited number of public IP addresses. To address this, NAT allows devices on a private network to share a single public IP address when accessing external resources, such as websites. This helps conserve the number of public IP addresses required, which is especially useful in light of the scarcity of IPv4 addresses.

Subnetting is the process of breaking down a larger IP network into smaller, more manageable subnetworks, or subnets. Subnetting enhances the performance and security of a network by dividing it into logical segments. Each subnet operates as an independent network but still communicates with other subnets within the same larger network. Subnetting is particularly useful in organizations with large numbers of devices that need to be grouped together based on geographic location, department, or function. By creating smaller subnets, organizations can reduce broadcast traffic, improve network efficiency, and better manage IP address allocation.

To understand subnetting, it is essential to first grasp the concept of a subnet mask. A subnet mask is a 32-bit number that helps determine the network and host portions of an IP address. It essentially divides the IP address into two parts: the network portion, which identifies the specific network, and the host portion, which identifies the individual device within that network. The subnet mask works by "masking" or blocking off the network portion of the IP address, leaving the host portion available for device identification. For example, in the IP address 192.168.1.10 with a subnet mask of 255.255.255.0, the first three octets (192.168.1) represent the network portion, and the last octet (.10) represents the host portion.

By modifying the subnet mask, network administrators can create subnets of different sizes to accommodate varying needs. The subnet mask also defines how many subnet bits are used to extend the network portion of the IP address. By borrowing bits from the host portion, administrators can create multiple subnets within a given IP address range. This process is done by applying a formula to calculate the number of available subnets and hosts for a given subnet mask. The more bits borrowed from the host portion, the more subnets are created, but this also reduces the number of available host addresses in each subnet.

An important concept in subnetting is the idea of CIDR notation (Classless Inter-Domain Routing). CIDR notation is a shorthand method for representing IP addresses and their associated subnet masks. Instead of writing out the subnet mask in the traditional form, CIDR notation uses a slash (/) followed by the number of bits in the network portion of the IP address. For example, the IP address 192.168.1.10/24 indicates an IP address with a 24-bit network portion, which corresponds to the subnet mask 255.255.255.0. CIDR notation simplifies subnetting and allows for more efficient use of IP address space.

Subnetting is essential for optimizing IP address allocation and managing network traffic. In larger networks, subnetting allows for more efficient routing, as each subnet can be treated as a separate entity, reducing the need for broadcasts across the entire network. Subnetting also improves network security, as devices in different subnets can be isolated from one another, making it more difficult for an attacker to gain access to other parts of the network. In enterprise environments, administrators often use firewalls or routers to control the flow of traffic between subnets, further enhancing security.

Subnetting also helps improve the scalability of a network. As networks grow and new devices are added, subnetting allows administrators to allocate IP addresses in a structured and organized manner. Instead of managing a single large network with a limited number of IP addresses, subnetting allows for the dynamic allocation of IP addresses across multiple subnets. This ensures that as the network expands, it remains efficient and easy to manage.

To calculate subnets, network administrators must understand how to work with binary numbers, as IP addresses and subnet masks are written in binary. Subnetting involves converting the IP address and subnet mask into binary form, performing bitwise operations, and then converting the results back into decimal. This process can be complex, but once understood, it allows for precise control over IP address allocation.

The transition from IPv4 to IPv6 has further impacted IP addressing and subnetting. While IPv4 provides a limited number of addresses, IPv6, with its 128-bit addressing scheme, offers an almost infinite number of addresses. Subnetting in IPv6 operates on similar principles as IPv4 but uses a larger address space, allowing for more flexible and efficient allocation. As the adoption of IPv6 grows, understanding the differences in subnetting between IPv4 and IPv6 will become increasingly important for network administrators.

IP addressing and subnetting are vital components of modern networking, enabling the efficient organization, management, and scalability of networks. By understanding how IP addresses work, how subnetting allows for more efficient address allocation, and how these concepts integrate into larger network design and security strategies, IT professionals can create and maintain robust and reliable network infrastructures. Proper use of IP addressing and subnetting ensures that networks remain organized, scalable, and secure as they grow and evolve to meet the demands of the modern digital landscape.

Chapter 20: Routers, Switches, and Hubs

In networking, devices such as routers, switches, and hubs play pivotal roles in enabling communication between devices and managing the flow of data across networks. Each of these devices performs distinct functions, helping to organize and route traffic in different networking environments, from simple home networks to large, complex enterprise infrastructures. Understanding how routers, switches, and hubs work is essential for anyone involved in the design, maintenance, and management of networked systems. These devices not only help direct traffic but also play key roles in optimizing performance, security, and scalability.

A router is a device that forwards data packets between different networks, typically between a local network and the internet, or between two networks within an organization. The primary job of a router is to direct traffic based on IP addresses, determining the most efficient path for data to reach its destination. Routers use routing tables, which are databases that contain information about the best routes for delivering data. These tables are updated dynamically through routing protocols, which allow routers to communicate with each other and learn about the network topology. A router is typically positioned at the gateway between different networks, often linking a private local area network (LAN) to the internet, and it is essential for network traffic management.

In a typical home or office network, the router acts as the central device that connects all the devices on the network to the internet. When a device, such as a computer or smartphone, wants to access a website, for example, the data request is first sent to the router, which forwards it to the appropriate destination. The router also receives the response from the destination and sends it back to the device. Modern routers also include firewall capabilities, which help protect the network from unauthorized access and potential threats coming from the internet. Additionally, routers often offer network address translation (NAT), which allows multiple devices within a private network to share a single public IP address when accessing the internet. This feature is particularly important as IPv4 addresses are limited, and NAT helps to conserve address space.

On the other hand, switches operate within a local area network and are responsible for directing data traffic between devices on the same network. Unlike routers, which work with IP addresses to route data between different networks, switches operate primarily with MAC addresses, which are unique identifiers assigned to network devices. When a device sends data on the network, the switch uses the MAC address to forward the data to the correct destination device. Switches are more efficient than hubs because they intelligently forward data only to the device that needs it, reducing the overall network traffic and minimizing collisions that can occur when data is broadcast to all devices.

Switches can be used to create network segments, allowing administrators to break up large networks into smaller, more manageable parts. This segmentation helps to improve performance by reducing congestion and ensures that network resources are allocated efficiently. In addition to basic functions, modern managed switches offer advanced features such as VLAN (Virtual Local Area Network) support, which allows for network isolation and better security. Managed switches also provide detailed monitoring capabilities, allowing administrators to track network traffic, identify potential issues, and implement quality of service (QoS) policies to prioritize critical traffic over less important data.

While switches are designed to efficiently direct traffic within a single network, hubs are simpler devices that serve as a central connection point for devices within a network. A hub receives data from one device and broadcasts it to all other devices connected to it. Unlike a switch, which sends data only to the intended recipient, a hub sends data to all devices, regardless of whether they need it. This makes hubs less efficient than switches, especially in large networks, as it increases network congestion and the potential for data collisions. As a result, hubs are typically used in smaller networks or older networking setups where traffic management is less of a concern.

Despite their inefficiency, hubs can still be useful in some environments, particularly when the goal is simply to connect a small number of devices in a basic network. However, as network demands have increased and technology has evolved, hubs have largely been replaced by switches in most modern networking environments. The key disadvantage of hubs is that they cannot manage network traffic intelligently, and the lack of segmentation and traffic filtering can result in performance degradation as the network grows.

Each of these devices—routers, switches, and hubs—plays a crucial role in different aspects of network performance and management. Routers are essential for connecting different networks, directing traffic between them, and providing access to external resources, such as the internet. They are particularly important in complex, multi-network environments, as they ensure that data is routed efficiently and securely. Switches, in contrast, are designed for use within a single network, directing traffic between devices with greater efficiency than hubs. They improve the overall performance of the network by reducing congestion and minimizing data collisions, making them ideal for most modern network setups. Hubs, while less efficient, still find their place in small or simple networks where performance and scalability are less of a concern.

The choice between routers, switches, and hubs depends largely on the specific needs of the network. In small home or office networks, a router may serve as the central device for both routing traffic to external networks and managing traffic within the local network. In larger networks, routers and switches are typically used together, with routers handling inter-network traffic and switches managing the flow of data within each network segment. In environments where performance and security are critical, managed switches offer advanced features like VLAN support, network monitoring, and traffic prioritization to ensure the network runs smoothly and securely.

Modern networking often combines these devices with additional technologies, such as firewalls, load balancers, and intrusion detection systems (IDS), to enhance security, scalability, and resilience. As networking requirements continue to grow and evolve with the increasing demand for high-speed data, cloud computing, and IoT devices, routers, switches, and hubs will continue to play an important role in shaping the network infrastructure of the future. Understanding the strengths and limitations of these devices is essential for building an efficient, scalable, and secure network that meets the needs of businesses, organizations, and individuals alike.

Chapter 21: Network Design and Topology

Network design and topology are essential concepts in creating a well-functioning, scalable, and efficient network. Whether building a small business network or designing an enterprise-level infrastructure, understanding how to structure the network's layout and its components is crucial for performance, reliability, and future growth.

Network design involves planning the components, devices, and links that make up a network, while topology refers to the arrangement or structure of those devices and links. The correct network design and topology can significantly impact data flow, security, and network management.

Network design begins with understanding the needs and requirements of the organization, the intended use cases, and the scale of the network. The first step is to evaluate the goals of the network, whether it is to connect a few devices within a small office or to handle the complex needs of a large enterprise. The design must account for current requirements while also providing scalability to accommodate future growth. It also requires careful consideration of factors such as performance, reliability, security, and cost-efficiency. For instance, if an organization plans to scale its network in the coming years, it must design the network to accommodate increased traffic, additional devices, and potentially more data centers or remote offices.

An important aspect of network design is selecting the right components for the network, which typically include routers, switches, hubs, and firewalls, among other devices. These components must be chosen based on the network's needs. For instance, high-performance servers, high-speed connections, and redundant links may be required for a data center network, while a small office network may only need basic routers and switches. A network designer must also consider the type of cables and connectors, whether using fiber-optic cables for long-distance, high-speed connections or copper cables for short-range, lower-cost applications. Proper device placement, cable management, and power distribution are also essential in the design phase to ensure efficient operation and prevent issues with signal integrity or overheating.

Once the components are selected, network topology is the next key consideration. Network topology refers to the physical or logical arrangement of the various devices and links in a network. It defines how the devices are connected to each other and how data flows between them. There are several different network topologies, each with its advantages and drawbacks, and the choice of topology depends on the size of the network, its intended use, and performance requirements.

One of the most common topologies is the star topology, where all devices are connected to a central hub or switch. This is the most common topology used in local area networks (LANs) because it is easy to install and manage. In a star topology, if one device fails, the rest of the network continues to operate without interruption. However, if the central hub or switch fails, the entire network can be disrupted. Star topologies are ideal for small to medium-sized networks because of their simplicity and ease of troubleshooting.

Another popular topology is bus topology, where all devices are connected to a single central cable, known as the bus. Data sent by any device on the network is received by all devices, but only the intended recipient processes the data. While bus topology is easy to implement and cost-effective, it is not as reliable as star topology. A failure in the central cable can bring down the entire network, making it less suitable for larger or mission-critical networks.

Ring topology is another arrangement where devices are connected in a circular fashion. Each device in a ring receives data from one device and passes it on to the next. This topology can be more efficient for certain data-heavy applications because data flows in one direction, preventing the collisions that can occur in bus topology. However, if one device or connection in the ring fails, it can disrupt the entire network. To mitigate this, dual ring topology can be used, where two rings provide redundancy, ensuring that if one path fails, the other path can still carry the traffic.

In mesh topology, every device in the network is connected to every other device. This topology is highly redundant, providing multiple paths for data to travel, which makes it extremely reliable. However, mesh topology can be expensive and complex to set up because it requires many cables and connections. It is generally used in high-availability networks, such as data centers or networks with critical applications that cannot afford downtime. The redundancy in a mesh network ensures that if one link fails, there are alternative paths for data to reach its destination, improving network resilience.

Hybrid topologies combine elements of different topologies to take advantage of their respective benefits. For example, a large enterprise network may use a combination of star and mesh topologies to connect different buildings or departments. Hybrid topologies allow for flexibility in meeting the unique needs of different parts of the network. For instance, the backbone of a network might use a mesh topology for redundancy, while individual departments are connected in a star topology for simplicity.

When designing the network, administrators must also consider the scalability of the topology. Networks must be designed with growth in mind, whether it involves adding more devices, expanding to new locations, or upgrading to higher speeds. Scalability is crucial because a network that is not designed to handle growth can experience slowdowns, outages, or even failures as more devices are added. A well-designed network will accommodate future demands without requiring a complete overhaul of the infrastructure.

Fault tolerance is another vital consideration in network design. A fault-tolerant network is designed to continue functioning smoothly even when one or more components fail. This can be achieved by introducing redundancy at key points, such as using redundant links, power supplies, and backup devices. In larger networks, this redundancy ensures that failures do not cause widespread disruptions, and traffic can be rerouted through alternate paths. Building redundancy into the design increases both the cost and complexity but ensures greater reliability and availability for critical systems.

Security is also a key aspect of network design. Secure networks are designed to prevent unauthorized access, mitigate risks from cyberattacks, and protect sensitive data. In the design phase, IT professionals must plan for secure access points, network segmentation, firewalls, and intrusion detection systems (IDS) to safeguard the network from threats. Network segmentation, achieved through VLANs or subnetting, ensures that sensitive data is isolated from other parts of the network, reducing the risk of unauthorized access. Firewalls and IDS systems monitor network traffic for suspicious activities and potential security breaches, providing an additional layer of protection.

As the network design progresses, management and monitoring systems must also be considered. These systems help administrators track network performance, detect issues, and ensure that the network operates smoothly. Network management tools provide real-time insights into traffic patterns, device health, and bandwidth usage, enabling quick detection and resolution of problems. Monitoring systems alert administrators to network failures, security breaches, or performance bottlenecks, allowing for rapid intervention and ensuring network reliability.

Effective network design and topology are critical in creating a high-performing, secure, and scalable network. By carefully considering the needs of the organization, selecting the appropriate topology, and planning for scalability and redundancy, network administrators can build an infrastructure that supports the organization's goals and adapts to changing demands. As technologies evolve and new devices and applications come online, the role of network design in ensuring the continuous operation of modern IT systems will only continue to grow in importance.

Chapter 22: Local Area Networks (LAN) vs. Wide Area Networks (WAN)

When it comes to networking, the terms Local Area Network (LAN) and Wide Area Network (WAN) are used to describe different types of networks that serve distinct purposes. Both LANs and WANs are integral parts of modern network infrastructures, but they differ significantly in terms of scale, function, and technology. Understanding the key differences between LANs and WANs is essential for anyone involved in designing, managing, or working within networked environments. These two types of networks have unique characteristics, advantages, and limitations that make them suitable for different applications.

A Local Area Network (LAN) is a network that connects devices within a limited geographic area, such as a home, office, or campus. Typically, LANs are confined to a single building or a group of nearby buildings, making them ideal for environments where devices need to communicate with one another and share resources over relatively short distances. A LAN allows computers, printers, servers, and other devices to connect to each other and share files, printers, and internet connections, providing a cost-effective solution for small to medium-sized networks.

The most common technology used in LANs is Ethernet, which enables devices to communicate over wired connections using copper cables or fiber-optic cables. Ethernet offers high-speed data transfer, and its reliability and simplicity have made it the dominant choice for LANs. In addition to wired connections, Wi-Fi has become increasingly popular for wireless LANs (WLANs), allowing devices like smartphones, laptops, and tablets to connect to the network without the need for physical cables. Wireless LANs are particularly useful in environments where mobility is required, such as in offices, libraries, and public spaces.

One of the defining characteristics of a LAN is its high data transfer speeds, which typically range from 100 Mbps to 10 Gbps, depending on the technology used. This high speed, combined with the relatively short distance between devices, ensures that LANs can support a wide range of applications, from basic file sharing and printing to more complex tasks like video conferencing, database access, and collaborative work. Moreover, LANs are typically private networks, which means that they are not accessible to the outside world unless explicitly configured to do so, providing a certain level of security for the devices connected to the network.

In terms of cost, LANs are relatively inexpensive to set up and maintain. The hardware required to build a LAN is widely available, and many organizations use off-the-shelf equipment like routers, switches, and access points to create their networks. The scalability of LANs is also one of their strengths, as it is easy to add more devices to a network as needs grow. However, as the size and complexity of the LAN increase, so do the demands on network management and maintenance. Administering a LAN requires ensuring that devices are properly configured, security measures are in place, and the network is optimized for performance.

In contrast, a Wide Area Network (WAN) is a network that spans a much larger geographic area than a LAN, typically connecting devices and systems across cities, countries, or even continents. WANs are used to link multiple LANs together, allowing devices in different locations to communicate as though they are part of the same network. The primary function of a WAN is to enable long-distance communication between networks, supporting applications such as internet access, email, remote work, and global communication.

WANs operate over public or leased communication links, such as telephone lines, fiber-optic cables, and satellite links, to connect devices that are far apart. Unlike LANs, which are often confined to a single building or campus, WANs require more sophisticated technology to ensure reliable communication across vast distances. The most common protocol used in WANs is MPLS (Multiprotocol Label Switching), which helps route data efficiently across different networks and ensures that traffic is prioritized based on its importance.

A key difference between LANs and WANs is their data transfer speeds and latency. While LANs offer high-speed connections, WANs are generally slower due to the longer distances data must travel and the increased number of intermediary devices, such as routers and switches, that manage the traffic. WANs typically have lower speeds than LANs, and the data transfer speeds can vary significantly depending on the type of connection and the distance between devices. Additionally, WANs tend to have higher latency, or delay, due to the longer physical distance between devices and the greater number of network components involved in transmitting data.

Security is another significant concern when dealing with WANs. Since WANs often involve connections over public networks or third-party infrastructure, they are more vulnerable to cyberattacks and data breaches compared to LANs. As a result, security measures such as encryption, VPNs (Virtual Private Networks), and firewalls are commonly used to protect the data being transmitted across WANs. These security protocols help ensure that sensitive information is protected from unauthorized access and that communication between different LANs is secure.

One of the main challenges of WANs is their cost. Setting up and maintaining a WAN is generally more expensive than a LAN because it involves connecting multiple LANs over long distances, often requiring the use of leased lines or high-bandwidth connections. Additionally,

WANs require more complex infrastructure and support, as well as advanced routing and network management capabilities. The cost and complexity of WANs make them suitable for large organizations or service providers that need to support widespread operations or provide services over long distances.

In terms of scalability, WANs have an edge over LANs, especially when it comes to connecting multiple locations across vast distances. A well-designed WAN can accommodate new locations as the organization expands, allowing for seamless communication between remote offices, branch locations, or even international offices. However, the scalability of WANs is often limited by the available infrastructure and the need for careful network management to ensure that the expanded network remains reliable and efficient.

While LANs and WANs serve different purposes, they are often interconnected to provide a seamless network experience for users. Many businesses have a LAN within a single office or building but rely on a WAN to connect their various offices and data centers. The combination of LANs and WANs allows organizations to operate efficiently, with local networks supporting day-to-day operations and WANs facilitating communication and resource sharing across a wider geographical area.

In summary, LANs and WANs serve distinct but complementary roles in modern networking. LANs provide high-speed, reliable communication within a limited geographic area, while WANs connect those local networks over larger distances, enabling global communication and resource sharing. Both types of networks are essential in today's interconnected world, and understanding their differences helps network administrators design efficient, scalable, and secure systems that meet the needs of organizations across industries.

Chapter 23: Network Protocols and Their Functions

Network protocols are the rules and conventions that govern how devices communicate with each other over a network. These protocols are essential for enabling data transmission, ensuring that the data sent from one device can be correctly received and understood by another, even if the devices are from different manufacturers or use different technologies. In the context of networking, protocols define the methods for transmitting data, addressing systems, error handling, encryption, and other vital aspects of data communication. Understanding network protocols and their functions is fundamental for anyone involved in network administration, security, or troubleshooting.

The Transmission Control Protocol (TCP) is one of the most widely used network protocols. It operates at the transport layer of the OSI model and is responsible for ensuring reliable data transmission between devices. TCP guarantees that data packets are delivered in the correct order and that none are lost during transmission. It achieves this by using a system of acknowledgments and sequence numbers. When a sender transmits data, the receiver sends back an acknowledgment to confirm receipt of the data. If the sender does not receive the acknowledgment within a certain period, it retransmits the data. TCP also manages flow control to prevent network congestion and ensures that data is sent at a rate that the receiver can handle. This makes TCP ideal for applications that require high reliability, such as web browsing, email, and file transfers.

Another crucial protocol is the Internet Protocol (IP), which operates at the network layer of the OSI model. IP is responsible for addressing and routing packets of data between devices on different networks. Each device on a network is assigned a unique IP address, which serves as its identifier. IP uses this address to ensure that data packets are delivered to the correct destination. The two most common versions of IP are IPv4 and IPv6. IPv4 uses a 32-bit address space, which allows for approximately 4.3 billion unique addresses. However, with the rapid growth of internet-connected devices, IPv4 addresses have become scarce, leading to the adoption of IPv6, which uses a 128-bit address space and provides a virtually unlimited number of addresses. While IP handles addressing and routing, it does not guarantee the reliability or order of data transmission, which is where protocols like TCP come into play.

At the application layer, several protocols define how data is exchanged between software applications running on devices. The Hypertext Transfer Protocol (HTTP) is one of the most widely known and used protocols on the internet. It is the foundation of web browsing, enabling the transmission of web pages and other resources between a client (such as a web browser) and a web server. HTTP defines how messages are formatted and transmitted, and how servers and browsers should respond to various commands. When you enter a URL into your browser, the browser sends an HTTP request to the server, and the server responds with the requested page or resource. While HTTP is essential for web browsing, it does not provide encryption or security features. For secure communication over the web, HTTPS (Hypertext Transfer Protocol Secure) is used, which is simply HTTP layered with SSL/TLS encryption to secure the data transmitted between the client and server.

Another critical application-layer protocol is the File Transfer Protocol (FTP), which is used to transfer files between computers on a network. FTP allows a client to connect to a server, browse directories, and upload or download files. It operates on a client-server model, where the FTP client requests files from the server, and the server responds by sending the requested files. While FTP has been widely used for many years, it transmits data in plain text, which can be a security risk. As a result, SFTP (Secure File Transfer Protocol) was developed to provide the same file transfer capabilities but with encryption, ensuring that sensitive data is securely transferred over the network.

The Simple Mail Transfer Protocol (SMTP) is another important protocol used for sending email across networks. SMTP works in conjunction with other protocols, such as Post Office Protocol (POP3) and Internet Message Access Protocol (IMAP), which are responsible for retrieving and storing email messages on mail servers. SMTP handles the sending of email from a client to a mail server and between different mail servers. Once the email reaches its destination server, POP3 or IMAP allows the recipient to download or access the email.

SMTP operates over TCP and relies on a series of commands and responses to ensure that email messages are properly delivered.

In addition to these protocols, there are also protocols dedicated to the management and configuration of network devices. The Dynamic Host Configuration Protocol (DHCP) is used to automatically assign IP addresses to devices on a network. When a device connects to a network, it sends a request for an IP address to a DHCP server, which then assigns an available address. This eliminates the need for network administrators to manually configure IP addresses for each device, making it much easier to manage large networks.

The Domain Name System (DNS) is another essential protocol for the functioning of the internet. DNS is responsible for translating human-readable domain names, such as www.example.com, into IP addresses that computers can understand. When you enter a URL into your web browser, your computer uses DNS to find the corresponding IP address of the web server hosting the website. DNS is essentially the phonebook of the internet, enabling users to access websites using easy-to-remember names instead of complicated IP addresses.

The Address Resolution Protocol (ARP) operates at the data link layer and is used to map a device's IP address to its physical hardware address, known as the MAC address. ARP is essential for devices on a local network to communicate with each other, as it enables the correct delivery of data packets by resolving IP addresses to MAC addresses. When a device needs to send data to another device within the same network, it uses ARP to find the MAC address associated with the destination IP address. If the MAC address is not already cached, the device will broadcast an ARP request, and the target device will respond with its MAC address.

Lastly, the Internet Control Message Protocol (ICMP) is used for error reporting and diagnostic purposes within networks. One of the most well-known uses of ICMP is the ping command, which sends an ICMP echo request to a target device and measures the response time. ICMP is also used by routers and other network devices to send messages about network conditions, such as unreachable destinations or network congestion.

In summary, network protocols are fundamental to the proper operation and management of networks. From ensuring reliable data transmission with protocols like TCP to enabling web browsing with HTTP and email communication with SMTP, each protocol plays a critical role in modern networking. By understanding the functions and purposes of these protocols, network administrators and IT professionals can design, manage, and troubleshoot networks more effectively, ensuring smooth communication across devices and systems. The continued development and evolution of networking protocols will undoubtedly play a key role in meeting the demands of an increasingly connected world.

Chapter 24: Introduction to Wireless Networking

Wireless networking has become an integral part of modern communication systems, revolutionizing the way we connect devices and access information. Unlike traditional wired networking, which relies on physical cables to establish connections, wireless networking uses radio waves to transmit data between devices. This technology enables users to access networks and communicate over a broad range of distances without being tethered to a specific location. Over the past few decades, wireless networking has seen significant advancements, becoming a ubiquitous feature in homes, businesses, public spaces, and mobile devices. Understanding the basics of wireless networking, its components, and the technologies that drive it is essential for anyone involved in IT or telecommunications.

The core of wireless networking is the use of radio waves to transmit data between devices. Devices that communicate over wireless networks, such as smartphones, laptops, and tablets, are equipped with wireless network interfaces that allow them to send and receive data using radio frequencies. Wireless signals are transmitted through airwaves, and these radio waves are regulated by various agencies around the world to ensure they do not interfere with other communications systems. In most countries, the regulatory body is responsible for allocating different frequency bands to various communication technologies, including wireless networking.

One of the most widely used standards for wireless networking is the Wi-Fi (Wireless Fidelity) standard, which is based on the IEEE 802.11 family of protocols. Wi-Fi is used to connect devices within a local area network (LAN), allowing them to communicate with each other and access the internet wirelessly. Wi-Fi networks are most commonly deployed in homes, offices, and public spaces, providing high-speed internet access to devices without the need for physical connections. Wi-Fi networks operate in the 2.4 GHz and 5 GHz frequency bands, with more recent technologies also using the 6 GHz band. The use of different frequency bands allows Wi-Fi networks to operate with varying levels of speed, range, and congestion. The choice of frequency band affects the network's performance, with higher frequencies offering faster speeds but shorter ranges, while lower frequencies provide better range at the cost of slower speeds.

The IEEE 802.11 standard defines the technical specifications for Wi-Fi, including how data is transmitted, how devices communicate with each other, and how network security is handled. Over time, this standard has evolved to support faster speeds, greater efficiency, and improved security. For instance, early versions of Wi-Fi, such as 802.11b and 802.11g, provided speeds of up to 11 Mbps and 54 Mbps, respectively. More recent versions, such as 802.11n, 802.11ac, and 802.11ax (Wi-Fi 6), support speeds in the gigabit range and introduce technologies like MU-MIMO (Multi-User, Multiple Input, Multiple Output), which allows multiple devices to communicate with the access point simultaneously, improving overall network efficiency.

Wi-Fi networks typically consist of two main components: the access point (AP) and the client devices. The access point is the central device that provides wireless connectivity to the network, transmitting and receiving data between client devices and the network. The client devices, such as laptops, smartphones, and tablets, are equipped with wireless network adapters that allow them to connect to the access point. The access point acts as a bridge between the wireless clients and the wired network, allowing devices to access internet resources, file shares, and other services available on the local network.

Wireless networking is not limited to Wi-Fi. There are other types of wireless communication technologies, such as Bluetooth, Zigbee, and cellular networks, each designed for specific purposes. Bluetooth is a short-range wireless technology primarily used for connecting devices like headphones, keyboards, and mice to computers and smartphones. It operates in the 2.4 GHz frequency band and is optimized for low power consumption, making it ideal for personal area networks (PANs). Zigbee is another low-power, short-range wireless technology used in applications like home automation, sensor networks, and industrial control systems. It operates in the 2.4 GHz, 868 MHz, and 915 MHz frequency bands and is designed to support devices with limited power requirements.

On a larger scale, cellular networks provide wireless connectivity for mobile devices, such as smartphones and tablets, by utilizing radio towers and base stations. Cellular networks operate over vast areas, ranging from local neighborhoods to entire cities and countries. The evolution of cellular technology has led to faster data speeds and lower latency, with technologies such as 4G LTE and 5G providing high-speed internet access for mobile users. Unlike Wi-Fi, which is typically used for local area networking, cellular networks are designed for wide-area communication, allowing users to remain connected as they move across large distances.

The security of wireless networks is a critical concern, as wireless transmissions are more vulnerable to interception and unauthorized access compared to wired connections. To address these concerns, wireless networking standards have incorporated various security protocols. WEP (Wired Equivalent Privacy) was one of the first security protocols used in Wi-Fi networks, but it was found to be vulnerable to attacks. It was replaced by WPA (Wi-Fi Protected Access) and later WPA2, which provide stronger encryption and authentication mechanisms. WPA3, the latest security protocol, introduces enhanced protection against brute-force attacks, better encryption, and improved privacy for open networks. In addition to encryption protocols, 802.1X provides authentication to ensure that only authorized devices can access the network.

Another challenge in wireless networking is interference. Since wireless networks rely on radio frequencies to transmit data, they are susceptible to interference from other devices that use the same or nearby frequencies. Common sources of interference include microwave ovens, cordless phones, and other wireless networks operating on the same frequency bands. To mitigate interference, modern wireless networking devices use techniques such as channel bonding, which allows multiple channels to be used simultaneously, and beamforming, which directs wireless signals toward specific devices to improve signal quality and reduce interference.

The range and performance of wireless networks are also affected by factors like obstructions and signal attenuation. Physical barriers, such as walls, floors, and metal objects, can weaken wireless signals, reducing the network's range and speed. In large environments, such as office buildings or warehouses, multiple access points may be required to ensure full coverage. Wireless mesh networks can also be deployed to extend coverage by using multiple access points that communicate with each other, creating a seamless network.

Wireless networking has transformed the way we connect and communicate, offering unparalleled convenience and flexibility. Whether it's enabling employees to work remotely, supporting smart home devices, or allowing people to access the internet on their mobile phones, wireless networks have become a cornerstone of modern technology. As wireless standards continue to evolve, we can expect even faster speeds, more reliable connections, and expanded coverage, further embedding wireless networking into the fabric of our daily lives. Understanding the technologies behind wireless networking, including Wi-Fi, Bluetooth, and cellular networks, as well as the challenges and security considerations, is crucial for those responsible for designing and maintaining these networks.

Chapter 25: Network Security: Best Practices and Threat Management

Network security is a critical component of any organization's IT infrastructure. As organizations rely more heavily on digital systems to conduct business, the need to safeguard networks against various threats becomes increasingly important. Network security refers to the measures and practices employed to protect a computer network from unauthorized access, misuse, modification, or denial of service. It encompasses a wide range of technologies, policies, and best practices designed to defend against cyberattacks, safeguard sensitive information, and ensure the continuity of network services. As cyber threats become more sophisticated, organizations must continuously adapt and implement comprehensive strategies to secure their networks.

One of the most fundamental best practices for network security is the principle of least privilege. This principle dictates that users and systems should only be given the minimum access necessary to perform their tasks. By restricting access rights to the bare minimum, organizations reduce the risk of unauthorized access and limit the potential impact of a security breach. This practice applies not only to users but also to devices and applications within the network. In a typical network, employees may need access to certain files, systems, or databases, but they do not require unrestricted access to the entire network. Ensuring that only authorized users and devices can access specific resources minimizes the attack surface and helps mitigate the damage caused by compromised accounts.

Another critical aspect of network security is network segmentation. Segmenting a network into smaller, isolated subnetworks (or segments) helps to contain potential security breaches within a single section of the network. If one segment is compromised, it does not necessarily mean the entire network is at risk. This segmentation can be achieved using virtual LANs (VLANs) or firewalls to create boundaries between different parts of the network. For example, an organization's internal HR system may be separated from the public-facing website, so even if the website is breached, the attacker does not gain access to sensitive employee data. Network segmentation also helps to improve performance by reducing congestion and controlling traffic flow between segments.

Firewalls are one of the most common and essential components of network security. A firewall acts as a barrier between a trusted internal network and untrusted external networks, such as the internet. It monitors and controls incoming and outgoing network traffic based on predefined security rules. Firewalls can be either hardware-based, software-based, or a combination of both, and they provide a first line of defense against unauthorized access to the network. Firewalls can be configured to block certain types of traffic, prevent access from known malicious IP addresses, and detect potential security threats such as denial-of-service attacks. For effective network security, firewalls must be regularly updated and configured to adapt to new threats and vulnerabilities.

Intrusion Detection Systems (IDS) and Intrusion Prevention Systems (IPS) are additional tools used to enhance network security. IDS monitors network traffic for suspicious activity and alerts administrators to potential security breaches, while IPS goes a step further by actively blocking or preventing malicious activity in real-time. These systems are essential for identifying and responding to threats before they can cause significant damage. IDS and IPS are often used in conjunction with firewalls to provide a layered defense against intrusions. By using multiple layers of security, organizations can create a more robust defense against evolving cyber threats.

Encryption is another cornerstone of network security. It involves converting data into an unreadable format that can only be decrypted with a specific key or password. Encryption ensures that sensitive data, whether it is transmitted over the network or stored in databases, is protected from unauthorized access. This is particularly important for safeguarding data in transit, such as emails, financial transactions, or personal information. Secure Socket Layer (SSL) and Transport Layer Security (TLS) protocols are commonly used to encrypt data sent over the internet, particularly in web browsing and e-commerce transactions. Additionally, Virtual Private Networks (VPNs) provide an encrypted tunnel for remote users to access the corporate network securely, ensuring that data transmitted over potentially insecure public networks is protected.

Regular patching and updates are essential for maintaining the security of a network. Many cyberattacks exploit vulnerabilities in software and operating systems, and one of the most effective ways to prevent such attacks is to regularly update software and apply security patches. When a vulnerability is discovered, vendors typically release patches to fix the issue. Organizations must have a process in place to quickly implement these patches across their network to prevent attackers from exploiting known vulnerabilities. This includes not only operating systems but also applications, firmware, and any other software used on the network.

Authentication and access controls are critical components of network security that help to ensure that only authorized users and devices can access the network. Strong password policies that require complex, unique passwords for each account are a basic but effective step in protecting network resources. In addition to passwords, organizations can implement multi-factor authentication (MFA), which requires users to provide additional verification (such as a fingerprint, token, or code sent to a mobile device) in addition to their password. MFA significantly improves security by making it more difficult for attackers to gain access to network resources, even if they manage to steal a password.

Security monitoring is essential for identifying and responding to security incidents in real-time. Organizations should implement continuous monitoring systems that can detect abnormal activity on the network, such as unusual traffic patterns or access attempts from unauthorized devices. This monitoring can be achieved through network monitoring tools, log analysis, and security event management systems. These systems can help identify potential threats before they escalate, enabling organizations to take proactive steps to mitigate risks. Automated alerting mechanisms can notify administrators of suspicious activity, allowing them to respond quickly and reduce the impact of a potential breach.

Employee training and awareness are often overlooked but are critical components of an organization's overall network security strategy. Human error is one of the most common causes of security breaches, and employees who are not trained in security best practices are more likely to fall victim to phishing attacks, social engineering, or other malicious tactics. Regular security training helps employees recognize common threats, such as phishing emails or suspicious websites, and teaches them how to handle sensitive data securely. Additionally, organizations should establish clear policies regarding the use of personal devices, remote access, and the handling of sensitive information to ensure that all employees follow secure practices.

Lastly, incident response planning is a key aspect of network security that prepares organizations for the inevitable possibility of a security breach. No network is entirely immune to attacks, so having a well-documented and practiced incident response plan is essential. This plan should outline the steps to take in the event of a security breach, including identifying the threat, containing the damage, and recovering from the incident. It should also involve communication strategies to inform stakeholders, legal authorities, and customers, if necessary. A rapid and well-coordinated response can minimize the impact of a security incident and help the organization recover more quickly.

Network security is an ongoing process that requires constant vigilance, planning, and adaptation. As new threats emerge, organizations must stay ahead of potential risks by implementing robust security measures and best practices. By focusing on principles such as least privilege, encryption, authentication, regular updates, and employee training, organizations can build a strong security posture that protects their network and data from evolving cyber threats. Effective threat management relies on proactive detection, continuous monitoring, and a well-prepared response to incidents, ensuring the network remains secure and resilient.

Chapter 26: Firewalls, VPNs, and Secure Connections

Network security is an ever-evolving field, and as cyber threats become more sophisticated, organizations must adopt robust measures to protect their data, devices, and communications. Among the most critical tools in a network security strategy are firewalls, Virtual Private Networks (VPNs), and secure connections. Each of these plays a vital role in safeguarding digital environments, controlling access, preventing unauthorized activity, and ensuring secure communication over potentially insecure networks. Together, they form a comprehensive defense mechanism against a wide range of cyber threats.

A firewall serves as a barrier between a trusted internal network and an untrusted external network, such as the internet. Its primary function is to monitor and control incoming and outgoing traffic based on predetermined security rules. Firewalls are essential for protecting a network from unauthorized access, cyberattacks, and other malicious activities. They can be deployed in hardware, software, or a combination of both, and their main job is to decide which traffic should be allowed into or out of the network. For instance, a firewall can block traffic from known malicious IP addresses or restrict access to specific ports that might be vulnerable to attack.

There are two main types of firewalls: network firewalls and host-based firewalls. A network firewall typically operates at the perimeter of a network, filtering traffic between the internal network and the outside world. These firewalls can be configured to block or allow traffic based on factors like IP addresses, domain names, and protocol types. Host-based firewalls, on the other hand, are installed on individual devices, such as computers or servers. They offer more granular control over the specific traffic allowed on a device and are particularly useful in protecting endpoints from threats that bypass network-level defenses.

Firewalls can be configured in different ways to meet specific security needs. For example, a stateful firewall monitors the state of active connections and allows only traffic that is part of an established connection. This makes it more secure than a stateless firewall, which simply checks each packet of data in isolation without considering the context of the connection. Another type of firewall is the application firewall, which works at the application layer and is designed to block or filter specific types of traffic based on application-level protocols, such as HTTP or FTP. Application firewalls are especially useful for preventing attacks that target specific applications, such as SQL injection or cross-site scripting.

In addition to firewalls, Virtual Private Networks (VPNs) play a crucial role in ensuring secure communication over the internet. A VPN creates a private, encrypted connection between a device and a network, allowing users to access network resources securely from remote locations. VPNs are widely used by organizations to allow employees to connect to the corporate network while working remotely, ensuring that data transmitted between the device and the network is protected from eavesdropping, interception, and tampering.

A VPN works by establishing an encrypted tunnel between the user's device and a VPN server. This tunnel ensures that any data sent over the internet is encrypted and cannot be easily intercepted by malicious actors. There are several different VPN protocols, each offering varying levels of security and performance. IPsec (Internet Protocol Security) is one of the most commonly used VPN protocols, providing robust encryption and secure key exchange mechanisms. OpenVPN is another widely used protocol known for its flexibility, scalability, and strong encryption. SSL/TLS (Secure Sockets Layer/Transport Layer Security) is commonly used for securing web traffic but can also be used for VPNs, offering secure remote access to internal network resources.

VPNs provide a significant level of security by masking the user's IP address and encrypting the data. This helps protect users when they are accessing the internet over unsecured networks, such as public Wi-Fi in coffee shops or airports. Without a VPN, data transmitted over these networks can be intercepted by hackers and used to launch attacks or steal sensitive information. By using a VPN, users can ensure that their internet activity remains private and secure, regardless of their location.

Another important aspect of VPNs is their ability to enable secure connections for sensitive communications. Secure connections are necessary for protecting data in transit, especially when transmitting sensitive information such as login credentials, financial data, or personal details. One of the most common protocols used to secure connections is SSL/TLS, which provides end-to-end encryption for data transmitted between a client and a server. This encryption ensures that even if the data is intercepted, it cannot be read or altered.

Websites that use SSL/TLS protocols are identifiable by the "https" prefix in their URLs, and the presence of a padlock icon in the browser's address bar indicates that the connection is secure. SSL/TLS is not limited to web browsing and is used in a variety of applications, including email, instant messaging, and VoIP (Voice over Internet Protocol) communications. The use of SSL/TLS certificates is vital in ensuring the integrity and privacy of data sent across the internet.

The security of a network is not just about implementing firewalls, VPNs, and secure connections; it also requires constant monitoring and updates to protect against emerging threats. Cyberattacks are becoming increasingly sophisticated, and attackers constantly find new ways to exploit vulnerabilities in networks and devices. As such, it is important for organizations to regularly update their security protocols, monitor network traffic for suspicious activity, and respond quickly to potential threats. Firewalls and VPNs, while effective, are not foolproof, and it is crucial to implement a layered security approach that includes intrusion detection systems (IDS), encryption, access control, and regular security audits.

Intrusion Detection Systems (IDS) help detect and alert administrators to suspicious network activity, such as unusual traffic patterns or potential attacks. IDS can be integrated with firewalls to provide a multi-layered defense that actively monitors for malicious behavior. Additionally, intrusion prevention systems (IPS) go a step further by automatically blocking harmful traffic, preventing attacks before they can succeed.

Maintaining a secure network also involves access control measures to limit who can access certain resources. This includes multi-factor authentication (MFA), which requires users to provide more than just a password to access sensitive systems. MFA can include something the user knows (like a password), something the user has (such as a smartphone app or hardware token), or something the user is (like a fingerprint or facial recognition). By requiring multiple forms of authentication, organizations can reduce the risk of unauthorized access even if a password is compromised.

Ultimately, firewalls, VPNs, and secure connections are essential components of a comprehensive network security strategy. They work together to protect sensitive data, secure communications, and ensure that only authorized users can access critical resources. As cyber threats continue to evolve, organizations must remain vigilant and proactive in their efforts to secure their networks. By continuously updating and improving security measures, organizations can protect their digital assets, maintain the integrity of their systems, and safeguard the privacy of their users.

Chapter 27: Cloud Connectivity and Hybrid IT Infrastructure

In the modern world of IT, businesses are increasingly relying on cloud technologies to enhance their operations, streamline their services, and reduce infrastructure costs. As organizations move toward cloud computing, the complexity of managing their IT infrastructure also grows. Cloud connectivity and hybrid IT infrastructure are two concepts that have gained significant traction in recent years, providing businesses with the flexibility to leverage the benefits of both on-premises and cloud environments. By connecting on-premises IT infrastructure with cloud services, companies can create a more dynamic, scalable, and efficient system that meets the demands of a constantly evolving digital landscape.

Cloud connectivity refers to the ability to establish seamless, reliable connections between an organization's on-premises systems and cloud environments. It allows businesses to access cloud services, store data, and run applications in the cloud while maintaining the ability to manage and control their existing IT infrastructure. The need for cloud connectivity is driven by the increasing adoption of cloud platforms, such as Amazon Web Services (AWS), Microsoft Azure, and Google Cloud, which offer a broad range of services from data storage and computing power to artificial intelligence and machine learning. These platforms are often viewed as cost-effective, flexible, and scalable solutions that enable organizations to meet their growing demands for computing resources without having to invest heavily in physical infrastructure.

Cloud connectivity is achieved through various methods, depending on the specific needs of the organization. One common method is VPN (Virtual Private Network), which establishes an encrypted connection between on-premises infrastructure and the cloud. VPNs ensure that data transmitted between the two environments is secure, preventing unauthorized access and mitigating the risks associated with sending sensitive information over the internet. This secure communication is vital for businesses that require consistent and reliable access to cloud-based resources while ensuring that their on-premises networks are protected from potential threats.

Another method of cloud connectivity is the use of direct connections, such as AWS Direct Connect or Azure ExpressRoute, which provide dedicated, high-speed, and low-latency connections between an organization's data centers and cloud services. These connections bypass the public internet, providing a more secure and reliable means of connecting to the cloud. Direct connections are particularly beneficial for businesses with high-performance applications or those that handle large volumes of data. These connections can also help improve the overall performance and consistency of cloud services, as they offer more predictable network speeds and reduced risk of congestion.

As cloud adoption continues to grow, many businesses are embracing hybrid IT infrastructure, which combines on-premises infrastructure with cloud services. A hybrid IT environment allows organizations to leverage the strengths of both public and private cloud environments while maintaining some of their traditional on-premises systems. This approach provides businesses with the flexibility to move workloads and applications between on-premises and cloud environments, depending on their performance requirements, cost considerations, and security needs.

Hybrid IT infrastructure is particularly useful for businesses that require the agility of the cloud but also need to retain control over certain aspects of their IT environment. For example, an organization may choose to keep sensitive data or mission-critical applications on private servers while using the cloud for less-sensitive applications or to handle temporary spikes in demand. This approach enables businesses to optimize their infrastructure costs by only paying for cloud resources when necessary while still maintaining control over their core operations.

A major advantage of hybrid IT infrastructure is its flexibility. By integrating on-premises systems with cloud services, businesses can optimize their IT resources, scaling up or down as needed based on changing business requirements. For instance, during periods of high demand, a company may choose to offload some of its computing tasks to the cloud, ensuring that its on-premises infrastructure is not overwhelmed. Conversely, when demand subsides, the company can scale back its cloud usage, reducing costs. This flexibility allows businesses to avoid the high capital expenditures associated with maintaining an over-provisioned on-premises infrastructure while still ensuring that they have the resources needed to meet their operational needs.

Hybrid IT environments also offer enhanced resilience and disaster recovery capabilities. By using both on-premises and cloud systems, businesses can ensure that their operations remain unaffected in the event of a failure in one of the environments. For example, if there is an outage in the cloud service provider's data center, an organization can continue operating using its on-premises systems or other cloud regions. Similarly, if there is a failure in the on-premises infrastructure, the organization can shift workloads to the cloud, maintaining business continuity and reducing the risk of downtime. This redundancy is particularly important for businesses that rely on constant uptime, such as e-commerce platforms or financial institutions.

However, the integration of cloud services with on-premises infrastructure presents several challenges. One of the key issues is ensuring that the cloud environment and on-premises systems can communicate effectively with each other. This requires careful planning and configuration of network connectivity, security protocols, and application interoperability. Businesses must ensure that their cloud resources are fully integrated with their on-premises systems, so that data and applications can be seamlessly shared and accessed across environments. This can involve setting up APIs, databases, or identity management systems that work across both environments.

Security is another important consideration when implementing hybrid IT infrastructure. While the cloud offers numerous benefits, including scalability and cost efficiency, it also presents security risks due to the fact that businesses are entrusting sensitive data to third-party providers. In a hybrid IT environment, security must be carefully managed to ensure that data is protected in both on-premises and cloud environments. This requires implementing strong encryption for data in transit and at rest, using firewalls to control access between environments, and applying security policies that ensure compliance with industry standards and regulations. Organizations must also be vigilant in monitoring for potential threats, including unauthorized access, data breaches, and other cyberattacks.

One approach to managing hybrid IT security is the use of cloud access security brokers (CASBs), which act as intermediaries between on-premises systems and cloud services. CASBs help enforce security policies, monitor traffic, and detect threats across both environments. They provide visibility into cloud usage and help ensure that sensitive data is protected, regardless of where it is stored or processed.

Cloud connectivity and hybrid IT infrastructure are becoming increasingly important as organizations seek to optimize their IT resources and adapt to the demands of the modern digital landscape. By combining the agility and scalability of the cloud with the control and security of on-premises systems, businesses can create a more dynamic, flexible, and efficient IT environment. However, the implementation of hybrid IT requires careful planning, integration, and security management to ensure that both environments function seamlessly and securely. As businesses continue to embrace cloud technologies, the ability to manage hybrid IT infrastructure effectively will be a critical factor in driving digital transformation and maintaining a competitive edge.

Chapter 28: Data Center Design and Management

Data centers are the backbone of modern digital infrastructure. They house the critical hardware that supports everything from websites and online applications to cloud services and big data processing. As the demand for data storage, computing power, and internet connectivity continues to grow, the importance of efficient data center design and management cannot be overstated. A well-designed and well-managed data center ensures that an organization's IT infrastructure operates smoothly, with minimal downtime, and can scale to meet future needs.

It also ensures that the facility is secure, energy-efficient, and able to handle increasing demands for bandwidth, storage, and computational power.

The design of a data center involves many complex factors that must be carefully planned and integrated. The first key consideration is the physical layout of the facility. This includes decisions about the building's location, the floor plan, and the physical space dedicated to housing servers, storage devices, networking equipment, and power supplies. One of the most important aspects of data center design is ensuring that the facility has adequate cooling systems in place. Servers generate a significant amount of heat, and if not properly managed, this heat can cause equipment to fail. Cooling systems, such as air conditioning units, liquid cooling systems, or evaporative cooling, are essential to maintaining optimal temperatures in the data center and ensuring that the hardware operates efficiently.

Another critical component of data center design is the power supply. Data centers require a reliable and uninterrupted power source to keep operations running 24/7. This is often achieved through a combination of uninterruptible power supplies (UPS) and backup generators. A UPS ensures that there is no downtime in the event of a power failure by providing immediate backup power to the data center's critical equipment. Backup generators are used to provide long-term power in the event of an extended outage. Power redundancy is crucial for ensuring high availability and reliability in a data center, especially when dealing with mission-critical applications or services that cannot afford downtime.

In addition to cooling and power, network connectivity is a fundamental aspect of data center design. Data centers require high-speed, reliable internet connections to ensure that data can be transmitted quickly and efficiently between servers and end users. The design of the network infrastructure within the data center must account for factors such as bandwidth, latency, and redundancy. Switches, routers, and firewalls must be carefully configured to ensure that data flows smoothly between devices and that the network is secure from potential threats. Fiber-optic cables and high-bandwidth connections are often used in data centers to provide the high-speed transmission required for modern applications, such as cloud services and real-time data processing.

Once the physical infrastructure of the data center is designed and implemented, the next critical step is management. Effective management ensures that the data center operates smoothly, efficiently, and securely. One key aspect of data center management is monitoring. This involves continuously tracking the performance of all systems within the data center, from the power supply and cooling systems to the servers and network devices. Monitoring tools provide real-time data on system performance, allowing administrators to identify potential issues before they cause major disruptions. For example, if a server is running hot, the system can alert administrators to take corrective action, such as adjusting the cooling system or replacing faulty equipment.

Security is another important aspect of data center management. Given the sensitive nature of the data stored in a data center, it is essential to have robust security measures in place to prevent unauthorized access. Physical security controls, such as biometric access and surveillance cameras, are commonly used to restrict entry to the facility to authorized personnel only. Additionally, cybersecurity measures, such as firewalls, intrusion detection systems (IDS), and encryption, are implemented to protect the data stored on servers from potential attacks. As cyber threats become more sophisticated, data center managers must stay ahead of evolving risks by regularly updating their security protocols and conducting vulnerability assessments.

Efficient capacity planning is also a critical component of data center management. As organizations grow, their IT infrastructure needs to scale accordingly. Data centers must be designed and managed to handle both current and future workloads. Capacity planning involves assessing the organization's computing needs and ensuring that there is enough power, cooling, network bandwidth, and storage space to meet those needs. This may involve provisioning additional servers, upgrading network infrastructure, or expanding cooling systems. Predicting future growth is a challenging task, but effective capacity planning helps to avoid performance bottlenecks and ensures that the data center can handle future demands without disruption.

Sustainability and energy efficiency are becoming increasingly important considerations in data center design and management. Data centers consume a significant amount of energy, and as the global demand for computing power grows, so does the environmental impact of these facilities. To reduce energy consumption and lower costs, many organizations are adopting green data center practices. This can include using renewable energy sources, such as solar or wind power, to reduce the carbon footprint of the facility. Additionally, data center operators are implementing energy-efficient technologies, such as LED lighting, high-efficiency cooling systems, and energy-efficient servers, to reduce power consumption and improve the overall sustainability of the data center.

Automation plays an increasingly important role in modern data center management. With the growing complexity of IT infrastructure and the need for greater efficiency, many data centers are leveraging automation tools to streamline operations. Automation can be used to manage everything from power distribution and cooling systems to server provisioning and software updates. This reduces the need for manual intervention and helps to ensure that systems are operating at peak efficiency. Automation also improves consistency by eliminating human error, which is a common cause of downtime and operational inefficiency.

One of the most critical aspects of data center management is disaster recovery and business continuity. Data centers must be prepared for unexpected events, such as power outages, natural disasters, or cyberattacks, that could disrupt operations. A comprehensive disaster recovery plan outlines the steps to take in the event of a failure, ensuring that the data center can continue to function or quickly recover. This plan may include data backups, replication of critical systems, and failover mechanisms that allow the data center to switch to a secondary system in case of an emergency. Regular testing of disaster recovery procedures is essential to ensure that the data center can respond quickly and effectively to any disruptions.

Effective data center design and management are essential for ensuring that IT operations are reliable, efficient, and secure. A well-designed data center can support the growing demands of modern business, providing high availability, scalability, and security for critical data and applications. Proper management ensures that the facility operates smoothly, from monitoring system performance to implementing security measures and capacity planning. As organizations increasingly rely on data-driven technologies, the importance of optimizing data center operations to support these needs will only continue to grow. A well-managed data center can play a crucial role in enabling businesses to leverage technology for innovation, growth, and success.

Chapter 29: Internet of Things (IoT) and IT Infrastructure

The Internet of Things (IoT) is rapidly transforming the way businesses, governments, and individuals interact with the physical world. By embedding sensors, software, and connectivity into everyday objects, IoT devices create a vast network of interconnected systems that collect, exchange, and process data. This network has revolutionized industries, providing new opportunities for automation, optimization, and data-driven decision-making. As IoT technology continues to grow, its impact on IT infrastructure becomes increasingly significant. The integration of IoT into IT systems presents unique challenges and opportunities, requiring organizations to adapt their network architecture, security measures, and data management practices to accommodate the ever-expanding universe of connected devices.

The fundamental concept of IoT revolves around the idea of connecting physical objects to the internet, allowing them to communicate and share data with each other. These objects can range from simple sensors and home appliances to complex machinery used in industries such as healthcare, manufacturing, and transportation. The real power of IoT lies in its ability to collect real-time data from the physical world and use that data to make informed decisions, automate processes, and improve operational efficiency. For example, IoT-enabled sensors in a factory can monitor machinery performance, detect potential failures before they occur, and trigger maintenance alerts, reducing downtime and improving productivity.

For IT infrastructure, the rapid proliferation of IoT devices means that networks must be designed to support a massive influx of data traffic. Traditional IT infrastructures were not built to handle the sheer volume of data generated by IoT devices, which can number in the billions. This has led to the need for more advanced network architectures that can handle the high volume, velocity, and variety of data generated by IoT devices. A robust network architecture must be able to support seamless communication between devices, ensure low-latency connections, and manage vast amounts of data transmission without sacrificing performance.

Incorporating IoT into IT infrastructure also requires significant updates to the networking protocols used to manage device communication. IoT devices often use specialized protocols that are lightweight and optimized for low power consumption, as many IoT devices run on batteries or have limited computing resources. MQTT (Message Queuing Telemetry Transport) and CoAP (Constrained Application Protocol) are two common protocols used in IoT systems. These protocols enable efficient data exchange while minimizing the bandwidth usage, which is crucial for IoT devices operating in constrained environments, such as remote locations or areas with limited connectivity.

Edge computing plays a pivotal role in addressing the challenges posed by IoT in IT infrastructure. With the massive influx of data generated by IoT devices, transmitting all this data to centralized cloud data centers can introduce latency and bandwidth challenges. Edge computing addresses this issue by processing data closer to the source of the data, typically at or near the IoT devices themselves. This reduces the need for constant communication with distant data centers and allows for real-time decision-making. For example, in autonomous vehicles, edge computing enables vehicles to process sensor data locally, allowing for immediate decisions, such as stopping for an obstacle, without relying on distant servers. The combination of edge computing and IoT significantly improves the responsiveness, efficiency, and reliability of connected systems.

However, as IoT devices proliferate, data security becomes a critical concern for organizations. IoT devices often collect sensitive information, such as personal health data, location tracking, and industrial processes. With so many devices communicating across networks, ensuring that this data is secure is paramount. Securing IoT systems requires a multi-layered approach that includes robust authentication mechanisms, data encryption, and network segmentation. Because many IoT devices are deployed in physical environments that may not have the same level of security as traditional IT systems, it is essential to implement security measures at every stage of the device lifecycle, from design and deployment to ongoing maintenance and updates.

The diversity of IoT devices and the environments in which they operate also introduces challenges in device management. IoT devices often vary in terms of their hardware, software, and communication protocols, making it difficult to integrate them into existing IT infrastructure. Device management platforms are essential for ensuring that IoT devices are configured correctly, updated with the latest software patches, and monitored for performance issues. These platforms enable IT administrators to manage large fleets of IoT devices, track their status, and troubleshoot any issues that arise. Additionally, automated management tools can help streamline the process of deploying and configuring IoT devices across an organization's infrastructure.

Data storage and analytics are also crucial components of IoT integration into IT infrastructure. As IoT devices generate vast amounts of data, organizations must implement systems to store, process, and analyze this data effectively. Traditional data storage solutions may not be sufficient to handle the scale of IoT data, requiring the use of more flexible, scalable systems, such as cloud storage or distributed data systems. In addition to storage, data analytics is critical for extracting meaningful insights from the data generated by IoT devices. Big data analytics platforms and machine learning algorithms can be applied to IoT data to identify patterns, optimize processes, and predict future trends. These insights can drive operational improvements and create new opportunities for innovation.

The integration of IoT into IT infrastructure also presents opportunities for automation and smart systems. By connecting IoT devices to enterprise systems, businesses can create automated workflows that respond to real-time data. For example, in a smart building, IoT sensors can adjust the lighting, heating, and cooling systems based on occupancy data, ensuring energy efficiency while improving comfort. Similarly, in supply chain management, IoT-enabled sensors can track inventory levels and automatically trigger restocking orders when supplies run low. This level of automation can improve operational efficiency, reduce human error, and provide more timely responses to changing conditions.

Despite the many advantages, the integration of IoT into IT infrastructure presents a number of challenges that must be addressed by organizations. The sheer scale of IoT deployments requires careful planning and investment in the underlying infrastructure to support the growth of connected devices. Additionally, the complexity of managing and securing IoT devices and the data they generate requires specialized expertise and tools. As the IoT ecosystem continues to expand, businesses must stay agile and be prepared to adopt new technologies, frameworks, and best practices to ensure that their IT infrastructure can support the growing demand for connectivity, data processing, and security.

The future of IoT will undoubtedly be shaped by advancements in 5G networks, artificial intelligence (AI), and machine learning. 5G will provide the high-speed, low-latency connections necessary to support the growing number of IoT devices, particularly in industries such as autonomous vehicles and smart cities. AI and machine learning will enable IoT systems to become smarter and more autonomous, making real-time decisions based on data without requiring constant human oversight. The combination of these technologies will further integrate IoT into the fabric of modern IT infrastructure, creating a more interconnected, intelligent world.

Chapter 30: High Availability and Load Balancing in IT Systems

High availability (HA) and load balancing are two essential concepts in modern IT systems that ensure the reliability, scalability, and performance of services and applications. As businesses increasingly rely on their IT infrastructure to operate critical functions, the ability to minimize downtime and optimize resource utilization becomes more crucial than ever. High availability ensures that systems remain operational even in the face of hardware failures or unforeseen disruptions, while load balancing distributes workloads evenly across multiple resources, preventing any single server or application from becoming overwhelmed. Together, these two concepts help create a resilient, scalable, and efficient IT environment that can adapt to changing demands and maintain continuous service delivery.

High availability refers to the design and configuration of systems, applications, and infrastructure to ensure that they remain operational with minimal downtime. The primary goal of high availability is to eliminate single points of failure, meaning that no single component of the system should prevent the entire system from functioning if it fails. To achieve high availability, organizations implement redundancy at various levels, including hardware, software, and network components. Redundancy involves having backup systems or resources that can take over in the event of a failure. For example, a high-availability architecture may include redundant power supplies, network connections, and storage systems that automatically activate if a primary system fails.

In high-availability systems, data and services are often replicated across multiple locations, ensuring that if one server or data center goes down, another can quickly take over. This replication can be done synchronously or asynchronously, depending on the level of consistency required. Synchronous replication ensures that data is written to multiple locations simultaneously, providing the highest level of data consistency but requiring more bandwidth and potentially introducing latency. Asynchronous replication, on the other hand, allows for data to be written to the primary location first and then replicated to other locations after a delay, reducing the impact on performance but with the potential for data inconsistency during the replication window.

One of the key technologies used to achieve high availability is failover. Failover refers to the automatic switching of services to a backup system when the primary system experiences a failure. Failover can occur at various levels, such as at the server, network, or application level. For example, in a web application, if one server becomes unavailable, traffic can be automatically redirected to another server in the cluster, ensuring that the application remains accessible to users. This type of seamless transition is critical for minimizing downtime and maintaining service continuity, especially in environments where users expect 24/7 availability.

Another important aspect of high availability is the use of clustering. In a high-availability cluster, multiple servers work together to provide redundancy and load distribution. If one server in the cluster fails, the remaining servers can take over its workload without interrupting the service. This clustering approach is commonly used in database systems, where multiple database instances are synchronized and work together to handle database queries. The cluster provides fault tolerance by ensuring that data is always available, even if one or more nodes fail.

Load balancing, on the other hand, is the practice of distributing incoming network traffic across multiple servers, ensuring that no single server becomes overloaded. Load balancing is crucial for optimizing resource utilization and ensuring that services remain responsive, even during periods of high demand. By balancing the traffic across multiple servers, load balancing helps prevent performance bottlenecks and ensures that each server is operating within its optimal capacity. Load balancing also contributes to high availability by ensuring that if one server becomes unavailable, traffic can be redirected to other servers without disrupting the service.

There are different types of load balancing techniques, including round-robin, least connections, and IP hash. Round-robin load balancing involves distributing incoming requests evenly across all available servers in a sequential manner. This method is simple and effective but may not account for variations in server capacity or load. Least connections load balancing, on the other hand, directs traffic to the server with the fewest active connections, ensuring that servers with higher capacity or fewer requests receive more traffic. IP hash load balancing uses the client's IP address to determine which server should handle the request, providing a consistent routing of traffic for each user. Each of these methods has its advantages and can be used in different situations depending on the application's requirements.

In addition to these traditional load balancing methods, global load balancing allows organizations to distribute traffic across multiple data centers or regions. Global load balancing enables businesses to ensure that their services remain available even if one data center experiences an outage. By directing traffic to the closest or most available data center, global load balancing improves the performance and availability of services for users worldwide. This type of load balancing is often used in conjunction with content delivery networks (CDNs) and cloud providers, which have multiple data centers strategically located around the globe.

Load balancers can be deployed at different layers of the OSI model, depending on the specific needs of the application. At the transport layer (Layer 4), load balancing typically involves distributing traffic based on IP addresses and port numbers. This type of load balancing is protocol-independent and is suitable for applications that use standard protocols such as HTTP, FTP, or TCP. At the application layer (Layer 7), load balancing can be more granular, involving the distribution of traffic based on specific application-level parameters, such as URL paths, cookies, or headers. This type of load balancing is more intelligent and can be used for more complex applications that require specific routing logic.

To achieve high availability and load balancing in modern IT systems, organizations often rely on cloud platforms and virtualization technologies. Cloud computing providers such as Amazon Web Services (AWS), Microsoft Azure, and Google Cloud offer scalable, distributed infrastructures that can automatically scale resources based on demand. These cloud platforms often include built-in load balancing and high-availability features, such as auto-scaling groups and managed databases, which enable businesses to easily implement these concepts without the need for complex infrastructure management. Virtualization technologies, such as VMware and Hyper-V, also play a crucial role in high availability and load balancing by allowing multiple virtual machines to run on the same physical hardware and be managed dynamically for optimized resource allocation.

In addition to cloud-based solutions, on-premises systems can also be configured to provide high availability and load balancing. On-premises load balancers are often used in conjunction with hardware or software-based solutions that can be customized to meet the specific needs of an organization's infrastructure. These solutions can range from simple, low-cost load balancers for smaller applications to more advanced, enterprise-grade systems designed to handle high volumes of traffic and provide enhanced failover capabilities.

High availability and load balancing are essential components of modern IT systems that ensure continuous service delivery, optimize resource utilization, and enhance the overall performance of applications and services. By implementing redundant systems, failover mechanisms, and intelligent load balancing techniques, businesses can achieve a level of resilience that allows them to maintain high levels of uptime and meet the increasing demands of users. The growing reliance on digital services and the increasing complexity of IT infrastructure make it essential for organizations to adopt best practices in high availability and load balancing, ensuring that their systems remain reliable, scalable, and capable of handling future challenges.

Chapter 31: Monitoring and Managing IT Infrastructure

Monitoring and managing IT infrastructure are two of the most critical aspects of maintaining a stable, secure, and efficient digital environment. As organizations increasingly rely on complex and diverse IT systems to drive their operations, ensuring that all components of the infrastructure work cohesively and efficiently becomes vital. Proper monitoring and management not only help detect and prevent issues before they become critical but also optimize performance, enhance security, and enable informed decision-making. With the ever-growing scale and complexity of modern IT environments, leveraging effective tools and methodologies for infrastructure monitoring and management has never been more important.

At the heart of IT infrastructure monitoring is the continuous observation of system performance. This includes monitoring the status of servers, storage devices, network components, applications, and databases, among other elements of the infrastructure. The goal is to ensure that these systems are functioning optimally, providing insights into potential areas of concern before they escalate into larger problems. For example, a server that is experiencing high CPU usage or low memory availability could signal an impending hardware failure or resource bottleneck. If this issue is not addressed in time, it could lead to system downtime or degraded performance, which can negatively impact business operations.

A comprehensive monitoring strategy typically involves collecting a wide array of performance metrics, such as CPU load, memory usage, disk I/O, network bandwidth, and response times. These metrics provide visibility into the current state of the infrastructure and help identify patterns that may indicate underlying issues. Advanced monitoring tools often use agents that are installed on various devices within the infrastructure to collect real-time data, which is then sent to a central monitoring system. This system can provide visual dashboards, alerts, and reports that allow IT administrators to gain a clear understanding of the overall health of the infrastructure.

One of the most important aspects of monitoring is the ability to detect issues proactively. Rather than waiting for users to report problems or for systems to fail, proactive monitoring focuses on identifying potential issues before they disrupt operations. This involves setting thresholds for performance metrics and configuring automated alerts that notify administrators when these thresholds are breached. For example, if a server's disk usage exceeds 90% capacity, an alert can be triggered to inform administrators to investigate and resolve the issue before the server runs out of storage. Proactive monitoring helps prevent downtime, reduces troubleshooting time, and ensures that IT teams can take corrective action before a problem affects users.

Network monitoring is another critical component of IT infrastructure monitoring. Given that modern businesses rely heavily on interconnected systems, any disruption to the network can have far-reaching consequences. Network monitoring involves tracking the health and performance of network devices, such as routers, switches, firewalls, and load balancers, as well as monitoring the flow of data across the network. By observing network traffic, bandwidth usage, and potential security threats, administrators can quickly detect performance degradation, unauthorized access attempts, or network congestion. Network monitoring tools can provide insights into the causes of network slowdowns or failures, helping teams identify whether the issue lies with a specific device, network segment, or external connection.

Another aspect of infrastructure management is capacity management, which ensures that IT resources are aligned with the current and future needs of the organization. As businesses grow and evolve, their infrastructure needs change as well. Without proper capacity planning and management, organizations risk experiencing performance bottlenecks, over-provisioned or under-utilized resources, and increased costs. By continuously monitoring resource usage and analyzing historical data trends, administrators can predict when additional resources—such as servers, storage, or network bandwidth—will be needed. Effective capacity management allows organizations to scale their infrastructure in a timely manner, ensuring that they have enough resources to meet demand without overspending on unnecessary hardware or services.

Alongside performance and capacity monitoring, security monitoring is a critical component of IT infrastructure management. Cybersecurity threats are becoming increasingly sophisticated, and it is essential for organizations to monitor their infrastructure for signs of malicious activity or vulnerabilities. Security monitoring tools can detect suspicious activity, such as unauthorized login attempts, unusual traffic patterns, or malware infections. These tools also provide real-time alerts, enabling security teams to respond quickly to potential threats and mitigate the risks before they cause significant damage. Intrusion detection systems (IDS) and intrusion prevention systems (IPS) are often integrated into security monitoring solutions, allowing organizations to detect and block malicious traffic or unauthorized access attempts.

Effective incident management is another crucial component of managing IT infrastructure. When issues do arise, having a well-defined incident management process ensures that problems are addressed quickly and efficiently. This process typically involves identifying the root cause of the issue, assessing its impact, and determining the best course of action for resolution. Incident management also includes documenting the issue and any actions taken to resolve it, which helps build a knowledge base for future reference. By responding quickly to incidents and minimizing the time it takes to restore services, organizations can reduce downtime and maintain business continuity.

In addition to real-time monitoring, data storage management is another key responsibility in managing IT infrastructure. As data volumes grow, organizations must ensure that their storage systems are capable of handling this growth while maintaining high levels of performance and availability. Storage management involves monitoring the capacity, performance, and health of storage devices, such as hard drives, solid-state drives, and storage area networks (SANs). It also includes implementing backup and disaster recovery procedures to ensure that data is regularly backed up and can be restored in the event of a failure or data loss. Automated storage management tools can help IT teams optimize storage allocation, reduce waste, and ensure that critical data is always accessible.

Automation is increasingly being integrated into IT infrastructure management to streamline processes and reduce human error. Automated tools can be used to perform routine tasks, such as software updates, system backups, and configuration management, without requiring manual intervention. Automation not only increases efficiency but also ensures consistency across the infrastructure. For example, software patches can be automatically applied to all systems, reducing the risk of missing important security updates. Similarly, automation can help manage resource allocation, adjusting the allocation of compute, storage, and network resources based on real-time demand.

Cloud-based monitoring and management tools are becoming increasingly popular as organizations shift to hybrid and multi-cloud environments. These tools offer the benefit of being able to monitor and manage distributed IT infrastructures from a central location, allowing for more efficient oversight of both on-premises and cloud-based resources. Cloud monitoring tools can provide visibility into the health of cloud applications, services, and virtual machines, as well as detect potential issues before they affect service delivery. Cloud management platforms also integrate with other enterprise management tools, enabling organizations to manage their entire infrastructure from a single interface.

Monitoring and managing IT infrastructure is an ongoing task that requires careful planning, attention to detail, and the right tools. By implementing comprehensive monitoring solutions, organizations can gain visibility into the performance, security, and health of their systems, enabling them to make informed decisions and take proactive steps to maintain optimal performance. Through effective management practices, IT teams can ensure that their infrastructure remains secure, reliable, and scalable, helping to meet the evolving needs of the business.

Chapter 32: Configuration Management and Automation

In the modern IT landscape, configuration management and automation are two crucial practices that significantly improve the efficiency, reliability, and scalability of infrastructure. As organizations adopt more complex and dynamic IT environments, the need for effective configuration management and automation solutions becomes paramount. These practices help streamline workflows, reduce human error, and ensure that systems are consistently deployed, configured, and maintained according to best practices. By automating repetitive tasks and ensuring that configurations are standardized, businesses can achieve greater agility and operational efficiency, while also enhancing security and compliance.

Configuration management is the process of maintaining the consistency and integrity of an IT system's configuration over its lifecycle. It involves tracking, managing, and automating the configuration of software, hardware, and network resources to ensure they are configured in a controlled and predictable manner. In the past, configuration management was often performed manually, which could lead to inconsistencies and errors. However, as IT systems have grown more complex and distributed, manual configuration management has become increasingly impractical. As a result, automated configuration management tools have emerged as essential for managing large-scale systems and ensuring that infrastructure is consistent across various environments.

One of the core goals of configuration management is to ensure that all systems, whether on-premises or in the cloud, are configured correctly and are in compliance with organizational policies and standards. This includes managing the configuration of operating systems, network devices, databases, and applications, as well as tracking changes to those configurations over time. Configuration management tools enable administrators to define the desired state of a system and then automatically apply and enforce that state across multiple devices. This approach eliminates configuration drift, which occurs when different systems or environments become misaligned due to manual changes or inconsistent updates.

Common configuration management tools such as Ansible, Puppet, Chef, and SaltStack have revolutionized the way configuration tasks are performed. These tools enable administrators to write infrastructure-as-code (IaC), allowing them to define system configurations in code, which can then be version-controlled and shared across teams. Infrastructure-as-code allows IT teams to automate the provisioning and configuration of resources, enabling faster deployment cycles and greater consistency in infrastructure management. These tools also enable declarative configuration, meaning administrators can specify the desired end state of a system, and the tool will automatically ensure that the system reaches and maintains that state.

The use of automation in IT operations has become increasingly important in recent years. Automation refers to the use of scripts, tools, or platforms to perform tasks that would otherwise require manual intervention. In the context of configuration management, automation is used to reduce the time and effort needed to deploy, configure, and manage infrastructure. By automating routine tasks such as patch management, system provisioning, and software installation, organizations can free up valuable time for their IT teams to focus on higher-level tasks, such as innovation and strategy.

One of the most common forms of automation in IT infrastructure is the automated provisioning of resources. With automation tools, IT teams can define the configuration of servers, virtual machines, containers, and network devices, and automatically provision them based on predefined templates. This eliminates the need for manual setup and ensures that resources are deployed consistently across different environments. Automated provisioning is particularly beneficial in dynamic environments, such as cloud computing, where resources need to be scaled up or down quickly to meet demand.

Another area where automation has a significant impact is in patch management. Keeping software and systems up to date is critical for maintaining security and ensuring optimal performance. Manual patching can be time-consuming and prone to human error, especially in large, distributed environments. Automated patch management tools allow IT teams to schedule, test, and deploy patches across multiple systems, ensuring that vulnerabilities are addressed promptly and consistently. Automation helps to streamline the patching process and reduce the risk of security breaches, while also improving compliance with regulatory requirements.

Orchestration is a related practice that extends the capabilities of configuration management and automation by coordinating the actions of multiple systems and services across an entire infrastructure. While configuration management tools focus on the individual configuration of systems, orchestration tools manage the flow of processes and tasks across multiple systems. Orchestration tools, such as Kubernetes for container orchestration and Apache Airflow for workflow automation, allow organizations to automate complex workflows, such as deploying and scaling applications, managing containerized services, and automating data pipelines.

The combination of configuration management and automation has profound implications for the speed and efficiency of IT operations. Organizations that implement these practices are able to rapidly provision and configure infrastructure, scale their systems to meet demand, and maintain high levels of consistency and reliability across their environments. The adoption of DevOps practices, which emphasizes collaboration between development and operations teams, has further accelerated the need for automation and configuration management. In a DevOps environment, automation and configuration management tools are used to bridge the gap between developers and operations, enabling faster deployment cycles and more reliable systems.

A significant advantage of using automation and configuration management is the improvement in system reliability. By ensuring that systems are configured correctly and consistently, the risk of configuration errors and downtime is minimized. Automation also allows for rapid recovery from failures, as system configurations can be re-applied or restored automatically in the event of a failure. In the case of cloud environments, automated configuration management ensures that instances and resources are consistently deployed and scaled based on demand, which enhances overall system uptime.

Security is another area where automation and configuration management play a critical role. By automating the application of security patches, hardening configurations, and ensuring compliance with security policies, organizations can reduce the risk of vulnerabilities and breaches. Configuration management tools allow organizations to enforce security best practices across all systems, ensuring that sensitive data and critical infrastructure are properly protected. Automation can also help in detecting and responding to security incidents by automatically triggering responses to certain events, such as blocking malicious IP addresses or initiating incident response workflows.

As organizations continue to embrace digital transformation, the importance of configuration management and automation in IT infrastructure will only grow. By adopting these practices, organizations can achieve greater agility, reliability, and security in their operations. The move toward infrastructure-as-code, continuous deployment, and automated workflows is enabling organizations to keep pace with the demands of modern technology while reducing the complexity of managing large-scale infrastructure. As the tools and technologies continue to evolve, IT teams will be better equipped to handle the increasing complexity of modern systems and maintain control over their infrastructure. Ultimately, configuration management and automation are not just about improving operational efficiency; they are critical enablers of innovation and business success in the digital age.

Chapter 33: Service Level Agreements (SLAs) in IT Infrastructure

Service Level Agreements (SLAs) play a crucial role in defining the expectations and responsibilities between service providers and clients in the context of IT infrastructure. They are formal, written contracts that outline the levels of service to be provided, the performance standards that must be met, and the consequences if those standards are not achieved. SLAs are especially important in IT environments where uptime, performance, and availability are critical to business operations. In the fast-paced and increasingly complex world of IT, SLAs provide clarity and assurance for both service providers and their clients, ensuring that both parties are aligned on expectations and outcomes.

An SLA typically includes several key elements, such as the scope of services, performance metrics, support procedures, and penalties or remedies in the event of service failures. The scope of services defines what is included in the agreement, detailing the specific IT infrastructure or services being provided. For example, an SLA might cover services such as server uptime, network connectivity, cloud storage, and security monitoring. By clearly specifying the services included, both the service provider and the client can avoid misunderstandings about what is covered and what is not.

One of the most critical aspects of any SLA is the performance metrics that measure the quality and reliability of the services being provided. These metrics often include uptime guarantees, response times, resolution times, and throughput requirements, among others. Uptime guarantees are perhaps the most common and vital metric in an SLA, particularly for cloud services, data centers, and web hosting. An uptime guarantee specifies the percentage of time that a service is expected to be operational, often expressed as a number like 99.9% uptime. This means that, for a service that guarantees 99.9% uptime, the maximum allowable downtime in a given month would be approximately 43 minutes. Higher levels of uptime, such as 99.99% or 99.999%, are often seen in mission-critical IT services where any significant downtime could result in substantial financial losses or damage to reputation.

In addition to uptime, SLAs may define response and resolution times, which set expectations for how quickly the service provider will acknowledge and address service issues or outages. For instance, an SLA might specify that the provider must respond to a support request within one hour and resolve the issue within four hours. These metrics are particularly important in environments where IT infrastructure is integral to business operations, and delays in addressing issues could have a significant impact on productivity or customer satisfaction.

Throughput requirements in an SLA may also be specified, particularly for network services. Throughput measures the amount of data that can be transmitted over a network in a given period, typically measured in megabits per second (Mbps) or gigabits per second (Gbps). SLAs that define throughput levels ensure that clients receive the level of bandwidth they are paying for and that the network infrastructure can support their operational needs.

Another important aspect of SLAs is the support procedures outlined within the agreement. These procedures specify the process for submitting service requests, obtaining technical support, and escalating issues to higher levels of support if needed. Effective communication between the service provider and the client is essential to ensuring that the IT infrastructure is running smoothly and that issues are addressed in a timely manner. SLAs typically include contact details for support teams, the availability of support (e.g., 24/7 or business hours), and the methods through which clients can reach support teams (e.g., phone, email, or ticketing systems).

An SLA also typically includes details on penalties and remedies if the service provider fails to meet the agreed-upon performance metrics. These penalties can vary depending on the severity of the failure and the terms of the agreement. For example, if the service provider fails to meet the agreed-upon uptime guarantee, the client may be entitled to service credits or discounts on future bills. In some cases, if the failure results in significant business disruption, the service provider may be required to compensate the client for financial losses. Penalties and remedies are designed to ensure that service providers remain accountable for their performance and that clients are compensated for any inconvenience or loss caused by service disruptions.

SLAs also serve as a basis for continuous improvement. By regularly reviewing performance metrics and comparing them to the targets outlined in the SLA, both the service provider and the client can identify areas for improvement. For example, if a service provider consistently meets the agreed-upon uptime guarantee but struggles with response times, the parties may decide to revise the SLA to include faster response times as a priority for future improvements. SLAs provide a framework for evaluating the effectiveness of the service being provided and can help foster better communication between the provider and the client.

One of the key challenges in managing SLAs is ensuring that both the service provider and the client have clear visibility into performance. This requires the use of monitoring tools and reporting mechanisms that track the relevant performance metrics in real-time. Many modern IT services, such as cloud platforms, web hosting services, and network providers, offer automated monitoring dashboards that allow both the provider and the client to view real-time performance data. These tools can help ensure that SLAs are being met and provide transparency into areas where service delivery may be falling short. In some cases, these tools also enable clients to submit service requests or escalate issues directly through the platform, further streamlining communication and issue resolution.

For IT infrastructure that involves multiple service providers, such as cloud services, third-party vendors, and internal IT systems, multi-SLA management becomes important. This refers to the process of managing multiple SLAs that govern different components of the overall infrastructure. Multi-SLA management ensures that all parties involved in the service delivery are aligned with the overall objectives and that the performance of each component is monitored and managed effectively. This approach is particularly important in complex, distributed environments where various services may be interconnected and dependent on one another.

Service Level Agreements are not just important for external providers but also play a role in internal IT operations. For large organizations with in-house IT teams managing critical infrastructure, SLAs can define the expectations for internal services and help set clear performance standards for IT support and system availability. Internal SLAs can help align expectations between business units and the IT department, ensuring that critical services are delivered according to agreed-upon standards.

SLAs also play a key role in ensuring compliance with industry regulations and standards. Many industries, such as healthcare, finance, and telecommunications, have strict regulatory requirements regarding data privacy, security, and service availability. An SLA can help ensure that both the service provider and the client meet these compliance requirements by defining the performance standards necessary to adhere to regulatory guidelines. The inclusion of security metrics, such as data encryption, access controls, and incident response times, in the SLA ensures that both parties are aligned on their responsibilities to meet regulatory demands.

SLAs are not just legal contracts but critical tools that define the relationship between service providers and clients in IT infrastructure management. By setting clear expectations, monitoring performance, and establishing penalties and remedies for non-compliance, SLAs help ensure that IT services are delivered reliably and efficiently. They provide transparency, accountability, and a framework for continuous improvement, all of which contribute to the success of the relationship between the provider and the client. Effective SLA management is key to maintaining high levels of customer satisfaction, meeting business requirements, and ensuring the resilience of IT systems.

Chapter 34: IT Infrastructure as a Service (IaaS)

IT Infrastructure as a Service (IaaS) has revolutionized the way organizations deploy and manage their computing resources. By providing on-demand access to computing infrastructure through a cloud-based model, IaaS allows businesses to scale their IT resources efficiently, without the need for significant upfront investments in hardware or data centers. This model offers a flexible, cost-effective solution for companies of all sizes, enabling them to focus on their core operations while leveraging advanced IT resources for various applications, from hosting websites to running complex data analytics. As organizations increasingly embrace digital transformation, IaaS plays a pivotal role in shaping the future of IT infrastructure.

IaaS is a category of cloud computing services that delivers virtualized computing resources over the internet. The primary components of IaaS typically include virtual machines (VMs), storage, and networking resources. With IaaS, organizations can provision and manage computing power, storage capacity, and network infrastructure on a pay-as-you-go basis, without the need to purchase or manage physical hardware. This eliminates the need for organizations to invest in costly servers, storage devices, and networking hardware, as the infrastructure is hosted and maintained by a third-party cloud service provider.

One of the key benefits of IaaS is its scalability. Traditional IT infrastructures often require companies to predict future demand and purchase hardware in advance, leading to overprovisioning or underutilization of resources. With IaaS, businesses can scale their computing resources up or down based on actual usage, ensuring that they only pay for what they need. If a business experiences a surge in traffic, such as during a product launch or a seasonal peak, they can quickly scale up their resources to handle the additional demand. Conversely, during periods of low usage, businesses can scale down their resources, reducing costs and improving operational efficiency.

IaaS also provides businesses with flexibility in terms of infrastructure management. Unlike traditional IT models, where organizations must manage and maintain their own hardware and data centers, IaaS allows businesses to access a wide range of computing resources from anywhere with an internet connection. This flexibility enables organizations to deploy applications, store data, and run workloads in a variety of environments, whether on public cloud platforms, private clouds, or hybrid cloud configurations. The ability to choose the most suitable deployment model for their specific needs gives businesses greater control over their infrastructure while also allowing them to avoid the complexities of managing physical hardware.

Another significant advantage of IaaS is the reduction in operational overhead. Traditional IT infrastructure management involves tasks such as hardware maintenance, software updates, and troubleshooting, which can be time-consuming and resource-intensive. With IaaS, these responsibilities are handled by the cloud provider, freeing up internal IT teams to focus on more strategic tasks. Cloud providers offer services such as automatic software updates, hardware maintenance, and security patches, ensuring that the infrastructure remains up to date and secure. This also means that businesses do not need to worry about hardware failures or data center issues, as the provider is responsible for ensuring the availability and reliability of the infrastructure.

IaaS also supports disaster recovery and business continuity. Traditional disaster recovery strategies often require significant investments in duplicate hardware and off-site storage. With IaaS, organizations can implement cost-effective disaster recovery solutions that leverage the cloud's scalability and redundancy. Cloud providers typically offer geographically distributed data centers, ensuring that data is replicated across multiple locations. In the event of a hardware failure or data loss, businesses can quickly restore their systems from cloud backups, minimizing downtime and data loss. Additionally, cloud-based disaster recovery solutions allow organizations to test and update their recovery plans more frequently, ensuring that they are always prepared for potential disruptions.

Security is a critical consideration for any IT infrastructure, and IaaS providers understand the importance of safeguarding sensitive data. Most reputable IaaS providers implement robust security measures to protect data and applications. These measures typically include data encryption, firewalls, identity and access management (IAM), and intrusion detection systems (IDS). Cloud providers also comply with industry-standard certifications and regulations, such as ISO 27001, HIPAA, and GDPR, to ensure that their infrastructure meets the security and compliance requirements of various industries. While the cloud provider is responsible for securing the infrastructure, organizations using IaaS must also implement security best practices, such as configuring firewalls, monitoring access controls, and regularly reviewing security policies to protect their own data and applications.

The cost-effectiveness of IaaS is another compelling reason for businesses to adopt this model. In a traditional IT environment, businesses must invest heavily in physical infrastructure, which involves not only the upfront costs of purchasing hardware but also the ongoing costs of maintaining, powering, and cooling data centers. IaaS eliminates these capital expenditures by allowing businesses to rent computing resources on a pay-as-you-go basis. This model is particularly beneficial for startups, small businesses, and enterprises with fluctuating workloads, as it allows them to access enterprise-grade infrastructure without the financial burden of maintaining physical hardware. By paying only for the resources they use, businesses can optimize their IT budgets and reduce unnecessary expenses.

In addition to cost savings, IaaS provides organizations with faster time to market. By eliminating the need to procure and configure hardware, businesses can deploy applications and services much more quickly. This is particularly important in industries where time-sensitive projects and rapid innovation are essential for staying competitive. For example, a software development company can leverage IaaS to quickly spin up virtual machines for testing new applications or launching new features, allowing them to bring products to market faster and more efficiently.

The integration capabilities of IaaS also enable businesses to connect their IT infrastructure with other cloud-based services and on-premises systems. Many IaaS providers offer a range of tools and APIs that allow businesses to integrate with other cloud platforms, such as Platform as a Service (PaaS) or Software as a Service (SaaS) solutions, as well as with their internal IT systems. This flexibility makes it easier for businesses to adopt a hybrid cloud model, where some resources are hosted on-premises while others are in the cloud. Hybrid cloud environments are particularly useful for organizations that need to comply with specific regulatory requirements or have legacy systems that cannot be migrated to the cloud.

The future of IaaS continues to evolve as cloud technology advances. With the rise of edge computing and the growing need for real-time data processing, IaaS providers are expanding their offerings to support edge deployments. Edge computing allows organizations to process data closer to the source, reducing latency and enabling faster decision-making. IaaS providers are increasingly offering edge computing capabilities, allowing businesses to build more distributed and resilient infrastructure that can handle the demands of modern applications such as IoT and autonomous systems.

As businesses continue to embrace digital transformation, IaaS will remain a vital component of their IT strategies. By providing scalable, flexible, and cost-effective infrastructure, IaaS enables organizations to adapt to the rapidly changing digital landscape, optimize their resources, and stay competitive in an increasingly cloud-driven world.

Chapter 35: Software-Defined Infrastructure

Software-Defined Infrastructure (SDI) represents a transformative shift in how IT environments are designed, deployed, and managed. Unlike traditional infrastructure, which relies heavily on hardware-based components and manual configuration, SDI leverages software to automate and abstract the management of servers, storage, networking, and other infrastructure components. This shift enables organizations to create more agile, scalable, and cost-effective environments that can respond quickly to changing business needs. As the demands on IT infrastructure continue to increase, Software-Defined Infrastructure is becoming a key enabler for businesses seeking to modernize their IT systems and drive digital transformation.

At its core, Software-Defined Infrastructure is about decoupling physical infrastructure from the software that controls and manages it.

Traditionally, infrastructure components such as servers, storage devices, and network switches required manual configuration and were tightly coupled with the underlying hardware. Each component had its own management interface, and making changes to the infrastructure often involved complex manual processes that could be time-consuming and error-prone. With SDI, these components are abstracted and controlled through software, allowing for a more streamlined and automated approach to infrastructure management.

In an SDI model, the infrastructure is virtualized, meaning that physical resources such as servers, storage, and network devices are presented as virtual resources that can be managed and allocated dynamically based on demand. Virtualization is a key enabler of SDI, as it allows IT teams to provision resources without having to worry about the underlying hardware. For example, a virtual machine (VM) can be created on a physical server without needing to manually configure the server's hardware settings. This flexibility not only simplifies the management of IT environments but also makes it easier to scale infrastructure up or down as needed.

One of the key components of SDI is Software-Defined Networking (SDN), which allows network administrators to manage network resources through software rather than relying on physical network devices and manual configurations. In a traditional network, routers, switches, and firewalls are configured individually, with each device requiring separate management. SDN centralizes the control of the network, enabling administrators to configure, monitor, and manage network devices from a single software interface. This level of abstraction provides greater flexibility and agility, as network changes can be made quickly and programmatically without requiring physical interventions.

Software-Defined Storage (SDS) is another integral component of SDI. Traditionally, storage systems were tightly coupled with hardware, making it difficult to scale or manage storage resources in a flexible and automated way. SDS abstracts the management of storage resources, enabling administrators to control and allocate storage using software. This allows for more efficient use of storage capacity, as resources can be dynamically allocated based on demand. SDS also provides greater flexibility by enabling businesses to use a mix of storage hardware from different vendors, making it easier to integrate new technologies into the infrastructure without being locked into proprietary solutions.

In addition to SDN and SDS, Software-Defined Compute (SDC) is an essential part of SDI. SDC virtualizes computing resources, such as processing power and memory, and allows for automated provisioning and management of compute resources. Through the use of orchestration software, administrators can quickly deploy new virtual machines or containers based on workload requirements, ensuring that resources are allocated efficiently and without manual intervention. This level of automation reduces the administrative burden on IT teams and accelerates the deployment of new services and applications.

One of the primary benefits of Software-Defined Infrastructure is automation. By using software to manage infrastructure components, businesses can automate a wide range of tasks that would otherwise require manual effort. This includes provisioning new servers, configuring storage systems, and deploying network devices. Automation allows IT teams to focus on higher-level tasks, such as optimizing performance, improving security, and driving innovation, rather than spending time on routine maintenance and configuration tasks. Additionally, automated systems can respond to changes in real time, ensuring that infrastructure resources are always aligned with business needs.

The agility offered by SDI is another major advantage. In traditional IT environments, making changes to the infrastructure could take days or even weeks, as hardware had to be manually configured and integrated. With SDI, infrastructure changes can be made in real time through software, enabling businesses to adapt quickly to changes in demand, market conditions, or business priorities. This agility is especially important in modern environments where businesses are under constant pressure to innovate and deliver new services quickly.

SDI also provides significant cost savings. Traditional infrastructure requires substantial upfront investments in physical hardware, which can be costly to purchase, maintain, and scale. With SDI, businesses can reduce the need for large capital expenditures by leveraging virtualization and automation to make more efficient use of existing resources. Additionally, SDI's ability to dynamically allocate resources means that businesses can optimize resource utilization, ensuring that they are only using the capacity they need at any given time. This pay-as-you-go model reduces waste and allows businesses to better align their IT spending with actual usage.

Improved scalability is another benefit of SDI. In a traditional infrastructure environment, scaling up often requires purchasing and installing new hardware, which can take time and result in over-provisioning. With SDI, scaling is achieved through software-driven resource allocation, allowing businesses to quickly adjust capacity in response to changing demands. This elasticity is particularly important for businesses with fluctuating workloads, such as those in e-commerce or seasonal industries, as it enables them to scale their infrastructure without making costly and unnecessary investments in hardware.

Security is also enhanced in a Software-Defined Infrastructure environment. By abstracting the management of network and storage resources, SDI enables more granular control over security policies. For example, network security can be managed centrally through software, allowing for consistent security policies across the entire infrastructure. Additionally, automation can be used to enforce security best practices, such as patch management, access controls, and encryption, ensuring that systems are secure and compliant with industry regulations.

While the benefits of SDI are significant, there are also challenges to consider. One of the primary challenges is the complexity of managing and integrating multiple software layers across the infrastructure. With SDI, businesses rely on a variety of software tools to manage networking, storage, and compute resources. Ensuring that these tools work seamlessly together and are properly integrated can require specialized expertise and careful planning. Additionally, as SDI environments grow in scale and complexity, managing performance and troubleshooting issues can become more challenging, requiring advanced monitoring and management tools.

Despite these challenges, the adoption of Software-Defined Infrastructure continues to grow as businesses recognize the advantages it offers in terms of flexibility, cost savings, scalability, and automation. As the demand for agile and efficient IT systems increases, SDI will play an increasingly important role in enabling organizations to build and manage infrastructure that can adapt to the needs of the modern business environment. By leveraging software to control and manage IT resources, businesses can create more resilient, dynamic, and responsive IT environments that support innovation and drive business success.

Chapter 36: Edge Computing and Its Impact on IT Infrastructure

Edge computing is a rapidly emerging technology that is reshaping how businesses approach data processing and IT infrastructure. Traditionally, data from various devices and sensors has been sent to centralized data centers for processing, where it is analyzed, stored, and then sent back to the requesting systems or users. However, as the number of connected devices and the volume of data they generate continues to grow, sending all this data to a centralized location for processing can lead to significant latency, bandwidth limitations, and inefficiencies. Edge computing addresses these issues by bringing data processing closer to the source of the data, enabling faster decision-making, reducing reliance on centralized data centers, and enhancing the overall performance of IT systems.

At its core, edge computing involves deploying computational resources and storage closer to the devices or "edges" of the network, rather than relying solely on distant data centers. This could mean placing computing power in local servers, gateways, routers, or even directly on the devices themselves. By processing data at the edge of the network, rather than sending it to a centralized server, organizations can significantly reduce the time it takes to analyze and respond to data. This is particularly important for applications that require real-time or near-real-time decision-making, such as autonomous vehicles, industrial automation, and smart cities.

One of the most significant impacts of edge computing on IT infrastructure is its ability to reduce latency. In a traditional cloud computing model, when a device generates data, that data must travel to a central data center, where it is processed, and then return to the device or user. This round-trip process can introduce delays, especially if the data center is located far from the device or if the network is congested. By processing the data locally at the edge of the network, edge computing eliminates the need for long-distance data transmission, drastically reducing latency and enabling faster response times. This is crucial for applications that require immediate action, such as medical devices that monitor patients' vital signs or manufacturing systems that need to make real-time adjustments to production lines.

Another key benefit of edge computing is its ability to optimize bandwidth usage. As the number of connected devices increases, so does the amount of data being transmitted across networks. Sending all of this data to centralized cloud servers for processing can quickly overwhelm bandwidth capacity, leading to congestion and inefficiencies. Edge computing helps alleviate this issue by processing and analyzing data locally, only sending relevant or aggregated information to the cloud for further processing or long-term storage. This reduces the amount of data that needs to travel over the network, freeing up bandwidth for other critical tasks and improving the overall efficiency of the infrastructure.

Edge computing also brings significant resilience and fault tolerance to IT systems. Traditional cloud-based infrastructures are highly dependent on centralized data centers. If one of these data centers experiences an outage or failure, it can lead to significant service disruptions for users across the entire network. With edge computing, the distributed nature of the infrastructure ensures that even if one edge device or node fails, the rest of the network can continue to function. For example, in a smart city, if a local edge server responsible for traffic monitoring goes down, other edge devices or servers can continue to monitor and manage traffic flow, ensuring that the city's infrastructure remains operational without disruption. This decentralization makes edge computing more resilient to failures and better suited for environments where downtime is unacceptable.

The rise of edge computing is also driving advancements in network infrastructure. As organizations move toward distributed computing, they require new ways of connecting edge devices to the broader IT ecosystem. This has led to the development of new network architectures that prioritize low latency, high bandwidth, and high reliability. Technologies such as 5G networks, for example, are being deployed to support the growing demands of edge computing. 5G offers much faster data speeds, lower latency, and greater capacity than previous generations of cellular technology, making it ideal for supporting large-scale edge computing deployments. The combination of edge computing and 5G networks enables the real-time data processing needed for applications like autonomous vehicles, industrial robots, and remote healthcare services.

Another area where edge computing is having a profound impact is in the realm of data security. By processing data locally at the edge of the network, organizations can keep sensitive information closer to its source, reducing the risk of data breaches or interception during transmission. In traditional cloud computing models, data is sent over long distances and often stored in centralized data centers, which can become targets for cyberattacks. With edge computing, data can be processed and stored in more localized, secure environments, reducing the exposure of sensitive information and enhancing privacy and compliance with data protection regulations. Additionally, edge computing can provide better control over access to data and applications, allowing organizations to implement stronger security measures at the device or network edge.

Despite its many advantages, edge computing also presents challenges, particularly in terms of management and integration. Managing a distributed network of edge devices can be complex, as each device or node may have different hardware, software, and security requirements. IT teams need to ensure that edge devices are properly configured, maintained, and updated, which can be more difficult than managing centralized cloud infrastructure. The complexity of edge computing environments often requires the use of sophisticated orchestration and monitoring tools that can provide visibility into the health and performance of edge devices across a wide geographical area. Additionally, integrating edge computing with existing IT infrastructure and cloud services can be challenging, as it requires seamless communication between edge devices, centralized servers, and the cloud.

The growth of edge computing also raises concerns about data governance and compliance. With data being processed and stored in multiple locations, organizations must ensure that they comply with regulations such as GDPR, HIPAA, and other data protection laws. Managing data across multiple edge locations requires careful planning and coordination to ensure that data is handled securely and in accordance with legal requirements. Organizations must implement robust data governance policies and tools to track where data is stored, how it is processed, and who has access to it.

Edge computing is transforming how businesses and organizations manage their IT infrastructure, offering significant benefits in terms of performance, scalability, resilience, and security. By moving data processing closer to the source, edge computing reduces latency, optimizes bandwidth, and ensures faster decision-making for time-sensitive applications. As the number of connected devices and the volume of data they generate continues to grow, edge computing will play an increasingly important role in meeting the demands of modern IT environments. However, businesses must also address the challenges associated with managing and securing a distributed infrastructure, requiring new tools, strategies, and expertise to fully leverage the potential of edge computing. As this technology continues to evolve, its impact on the IT landscape will be profound, reshaping how businesses operate and interact with the digital world.

Chapter 37: The Role of APIs in IT Infrastructure

Application Programming Interfaces (APIs) have become a cornerstone of modern IT infrastructure, enabling the integration, communication, and interaction of various software applications, services, and systems. In an increasingly interconnected world, APIs serve as the bridges that connect disparate systems, allowing them to share data and functionality efficiently. The role of APIs in IT infrastructure has grown significantly over the years, as businesses and organizations increasingly rely on a combination of internal and external services to power their digital operations. APIs provide the flexibility, scalability, and interoperability necessary to create agile, dynamic, and responsive infrastructures that can meet the evolving needs of businesses.

At their core, APIs are defined sets of rules and protocols that enable different software components to communicate with one another. They allow applications to send requests and receive responses, enabling data and functionality to be shared between systems without the need for direct access to their internal workings. This abstraction layer simplifies interactions between systems and makes it easier to integrate new features, services, and technologies into existing infrastructures. For example, APIs allow organizations to connect their on-premises IT systems with cloud services, third-party applications, and external databases, enabling seamless data exchange and functionality without disrupting the underlying infrastructure.

APIs are essential in today's IT environments because they enable the integration of diverse systems and applications. In the past, organizations often relied on monolithic applications and on-premises systems that were tightly coupled and difficult to integrate. As the demand for cloud services, microservices, and hybrid IT environments has grown, businesses need a way to ensure that their systems can communicate and share data across different environments. APIs facilitate this integration by providing standardized communication protocols and data formats, allowing systems built on different technologies to interact with one another. Whether integrating third-party payment gateways, linking customer relationship management (CRM) systems with marketing tools, or connecting microservices in a cloud-native architecture, APIs are the fundamental building blocks of modern IT ecosystems.

One of the primary benefits of APIs is the automation they enable within IT infrastructures. By using APIs to connect various systems, organizations can automate workflows, reduce manual intervention, and streamline operations. For example, APIs can be used to automatically provision virtual machines in a cloud environment, trigger data backups, or synchronize customer data between internal applications and external platforms. Automation through APIs not only saves time and effort but also helps reduce human errors and ensures more consistent, reliable operations. This is especially important in large-scale IT environments where the complexity and volume of operations can make manual processes inefficient and error-prone.

The scalability that APIs provide is another crucial aspect of modern IT infrastructure. APIs allow businesses to expand and evolve their systems by enabling the seamless addition of new services, features, or capabilities. Instead of requiring significant changes to the underlying infrastructure or application code, APIs allow businesses to extend their systems with minimal disruption. For instance, as a business grows and its IT infrastructure needs to handle more data or traffic, APIs can be used to integrate new services or scale existing ones. This scalability is particularly important in cloud-based environments, where resources are allocated dynamically based on demand. APIs provide the flexibility to scale both horizontally and vertically, depending on the needs of the business.

APIs are also key enablers of innovation in IT infrastructure. By providing access to a wide range of third-party services and technologies, APIs empower organizations to experiment with new ideas and quickly incorporate new capabilities into their systems. This fosters a more agile development environment, where new features and services can be developed, tested, and deployed rapidly. For example, APIs allow developers to integrate artificial intelligence (AI), machine learning (ML), and data analytics tools into their applications without needing to build these complex capabilities from scratch. By tapping into external services and platforms through APIs, businesses can leverage cutting-edge technologies and stay competitive in a fast-paced digital landscape.

Security is a crucial consideration when working with APIs in IT infrastructure. APIs provide powerful capabilities for integrating and automating systems, but they also introduce security risks. Since APIs are often exposed to the internet, they can become vulnerable to attacks such as unauthorized access, data breaches, and denial-of-service attacks. Therefore, securing APIs is essential for protecting sensitive data and ensuring the integrity of the infrastructure.

Organizations must implement strong security practices, such as authentication and authorization mechanisms, to ensure that only authorized users and systems can access the APIs. Techniques like OAuth and API keys are commonly used to control access and protect API endpoints. Additionally, encryption should be used to protect data transmitted via APIs, especially when dealing with sensitive information.

APIs also facilitate monitoring and management of IT infrastructure. By tracking API calls, responses, and performance metrics, organizations can gain insights into the health and performance of their systems. API management platforms provide tools for monitoring API usage, detecting anomalies, and ensuring that APIs are performing as expected. These tools can help identify performance bottlenecks, track the status of third-party services, and provide analytics that inform decisions about system optimization. In complex, distributed IT environments, where multiple services and systems are interacting through APIs, monitoring and managing API performance is crucial for maintaining the overall health and efficiency of the infrastructure.

Another important aspect of APIs in IT infrastructure is their role in enabling cloud-native architectures. As businesses increasingly move to the cloud, APIs play a central role in enabling the development of cloud-native applications and microservices. Cloud-native applications are designed to be scalable, flexible, and resilient, and they rely on APIs to interact with cloud resources, databases, and other services. Microservices, in particular, use APIs to communicate with each other and coordinate the functions of a larger application. This architecture enables businesses to build modular, independently scalable applications that can be easily maintained and updated. APIs are the glue that holds together these distributed services, ensuring that they can work together seamlessly in a cloud-based environment.

APIs also support the concept of DevOps by facilitating continuous integration (CI) and continuous deployment (CD) pipelines. In a DevOps environment, APIs are used to automate the process of building, testing, and deploying software. For example, APIs can be used to integrate version control systems with build tools, trigger automated testing, and deploy code to production environments. This level of automation improves the efficiency of software development, reduces the risk of errors, and ensures that changes can be deployed quickly and consistently.

The growing importance of APIs in IT infrastructure is also driving the evolution of API governance. As organizations rely more heavily on APIs, managing them effectively becomes critical to maintaining control over how systems interact. API governance involves defining policies and standards for API development, usage, security, and performance. It ensures that APIs are well-documented, secure, and adhere to industry standards, while also providing visibility and control over API consumption across the organization.

APIs have become an indispensable element of modern IT infrastructure, driving efficiency, scalability, and innovation. They enable organizations to integrate disparate systems, automate processes, and quickly scale their operations in response to changing demands. With the increasing reliance on cloud services, microservices, and automation, the role of APIs in IT infrastructure will only continue to grow, providing businesses with the flexibility and agility they need to remain competitive in an increasingly interconnected world.

Chapter 38: Security in IT Infrastructure: Risk Assessment and Mitigation

In today's interconnected digital world, securing IT infrastructure has become a critical concern for businesses of all sizes. The rapid growth of technology, the increasing reliance on cloud computing, and the surge in cyberattacks have made it essential for organizations to proactively assess and mitigate risks associated with their IT infrastructure. Effective security is not just about protecting data but also ensuring the availability, integrity, and functionality of critical systems that support business operations. Risk assessment and mitigation are the foundational practices for safeguarding IT infrastructure, enabling organizations to identify potential threats, evaluate their impact, and implement strategies to reduce or eliminate risks before they can cause significant harm.

Risk assessment is the process of identifying, analyzing, and evaluating potential security threats to an organization's IT infrastructure. It begins with a comprehensive understanding of the infrastructure itself, including all hardware, software, networks, and data components that make up the system. This knowledge allows businesses to identify the assets that need protection and the potential vulnerabilities that could be exploited by cybercriminals, hackers, or malicious insiders. During the risk assessment process, organizations must consider a variety of factors, including the type of data they store, the sensitivity of that data, and the potential consequences of a breach. The risk assessment process is iterative, as it requires continuous monitoring and adjustment to address new and emerging threats.

Once risks have been identified, the next step is to evaluate the likelihood and impact of each threat. This involves determining how likely it is that a given threat will exploit a vulnerability and what the consequences would be if that threat materializes. For example, if a company stores sensitive customer information, a data breach could have severe financial, legal, and reputational consequences. On the other hand, a relatively low-impact threat, such as a temporary system outage, might be less of a concern. By evaluating both the likelihood and the potential impact of each risk, organizations can prioritize which risks need to be addressed first and which ones can be monitored or mitigated over time.

The process of risk assessment also involves considering the organization's existing security measures and how well they are able to mitigate the identified risks. A company may already have strong encryption protocols in place for protecting sensitive data, but it may not have a comprehensive incident response plan for responding to a breach. Similarly, a business may have robust firewalls protecting its network perimeter but may be vulnerable to insider threats. Understanding the effectiveness of current security measures helps determine whether they are sufficient to manage the risks or if additional security controls are needed.

Once the risks have been assessed and prioritized, the next step is risk mitigation, which involves implementing measures to reduce or eliminate the identified threats. Risk mitigation strategies vary depending on the nature of the risks and the available resources. One of the most common risk mitigation strategies is to implement preventive controls that block or limit the likelihood of a risk occurring. For example, installing firewalls and intrusion detection systems (IDS) can prevent unauthorized access to the network, while encryption can protect sensitive data from being compromised during transmission or storage. Access controls such as multi-factor authentication (MFA) can also mitigate the risk of unauthorized users gaining access to critical systems and data.

In addition to preventive controls, organizations must also implement detective controls that help identify and respond to security incidents once they have occurred. These controls include monitoring systems, logging mechanisms, and audit trails that provide real-time visibility into network traffic and system activities. By monitoring for suspicious activity, organizations can quickly detect potential breaches or vulnerabilities and take immediate action to mitigate the impact. Detective controls also play a crucial role in ensuring compliance with industry regulations, such as GDPR or HIPAA, by providing a record of who accessed what data and when.

While preventive and detective controls are essential for reducing risks, corrective controls are equally important in mitigating the impact of security incidents. Corrective controls focus on minimizing the damage caused by a breach and recovering from it as quickly as possible. For example, businesses should have an incident response plan that outlines the steps to take in the event of a cyberattack, including how to isolate affected systems, communicate with stakeholders, and restore services. In the case of a data breach, corrective controls might involve restoring lost data from backups, notifying affected customers, and implementing stronger security measures to prevent future breaches. An effective incident response plan ensures that businesses can recover from security incidents with minimal downtime and financial loss.

Another key aspect of risk mitigation is business continuity planning and disaster recovery. These plans ensure that critical systems and services can continue to operate, even in the event of a significant security incident or other disruption. Business continuity planning involves identifying the most critical business functions and ensuring that they can be maintained under various scenarios, such as a cyberattack, hardware failure, or natural disaster. Disaster recovery, on the other hand, focuses on restoring IT systems and data after an incident has occurred. Both business continuity and disaster recovery planning require regular testing and updating to ensure that organizations can respond effectively to unforeseen events.

Organizations must also consider the third-party risks that come with relying on external vendors and service providers. Many businesses today use cloud services, software-as-a-service (SaaS) platforms, and other third-party solutions to run critical applications. While these services can provide significant benefits, they also introduce additional risks, such as the potential for data breaches, service outages, or compliance violations. It is essential for organizations to assess the security practices and performance of their third-party vendors before entering into contracts and to ensure that the vendor's security measures align with the organization's requirements. This can involve conducting regular audits, reviewing security certifications, and ensuring that clear data protection agreements are in place.

In addition to mitigating risks, businesses must also focus on creating a security-aware culture within the organization. Employees are often the first line of defense against cyberattacks, and their actions can have a significant impact on the overall security posture of the organization. Organizations should provide ongoing security training and awareness programs to educate employees about common threats, such as phishing attacks, social engineering, and malware. Employees should also be encouraged to report suspicious activities and follow best practices for securing passwords and devices. By fostering a culture of security awareness, organizations can reduce the risk of human error and strengthen their overall security posture.

As businesses increasingly rely on IT systems to operate, the need for effective security risk assessment and mitigation strategies becomes even more critical. By continuously assessing potential risks, implementing preventive, detective, and corrective controls, and ensuring that security practices are integrated into every aspect of the organization, businesses can protect their IT infrastructure from a wide range of threats. The evolving nature of cybersecurity threats means that risk management is an ongoing process that requires constant vigilance and adaptation. The ability to identify, assess, and mitigate risks proactively is the key to safeguarding critical systems, maintaining compliance, and ensuring business continuity in an increasingly digital world.

Chapter 39: Compliance and Regulatory Considerations for IT Infrastructure

In the modern business landscape, compliance and regulatory considerations have become an integral part of managing IT infrastructure. Organizations today face an increasingly complex and dynamic regulatory environment, with laws and standards designed to safeguard data, protect privacy, and ensure security. These regulations can vary greatly depending on the industry, geographic location, and the type of data an organization handles. As IT infrastructure plays a central role in supporting the storage, processing, and transmission of data, ensuring compliance with applicable laws and regulations is critical to avoid penalties, legal liabilities, and reputational damage. Furthermore, maintaining compliance helps organizations foster trust with customers, partners, and stakeholders, demonstrating that they are committed to safeguarding sensitive information and upholding the highest standards of security and privacy.

The importance of compliance in IT infrastructure cannot be overstated, as the consequences of failing to meet regulatory requirements can be severe. Compliance helps organizations address various risks, including data breaches, unauthorized access to systems, and improper handling of sensitive data. These issues not only expose organizations to financial penalties but can also lead to a loss of customer confidence and damage to their brand reputation. Regulatory requirements also serve to guide organizations in implementing best practices for security, risk management, and operational efficiency. By adhering to regulatory frameworks, organizations can better manage the risks associated with their IT infrastructure while ensuring that they meet industry-specific standards for data protection and operational transparency.

One of the key regulatory frameworks that organizations must consider when managing IT infrastructure is the General Data Protection Regulation (GDPR). Enforced by the European Union, the GDPR imposes strict rules on how organizations handle the personal data of EU citizens. GDPR applies to any company, regardless of its location, that processes personal data of individuals within the EU. Under GDPR, organizations are required to obtain explicit consent from individuals before collecting their data, ensure that data is stored securely, and provide individuals with the right to access, correct, and delete their data. The regulation also mandates that companies report data breaches within 72 hours of discovering them and implement robust security measures to protect data from unauthorized access. GDPR has had a global impact, prompting companies worldwide to reassess their data handling practices and invest in more secure IT infrastructure.

In addition to GDPR, organizations in certain industries must also comply with industry-specific regulations, such as Health Insurance Portability and Accountability Act (HIPAA) in healthcare, Payment Card Industry Data Security Standard (PCI DSS) in finance, and Federal Information Security Management Act (FISMA) for government agencies. These regulations set standards for how organizations must protect sensitive data within their respective sectors, and non-compliance can lead to heavy fines and operational restrictions. For example, HIPAA mandates strict safeguards for electronic health records (EHRs), ensuring that patient information is protected both at rest and in transit. PCI DSS, on the other hand, outlines requirements for the protection of credit card information, including encryption, access controls, and secure storage methods. FISMA requires federal agencies and contractors to implement robust security frameworks to protect government data and systems from cyber threats.

Data sovereignty is another important consideration in compliance and regulatory frameworks, especially for global organizations that operate in multiple countries or regions. Data sovereignty refers to the legal restrictions that govern where data can be stored and processed based on the country in which it resides. Many countries have data protection laws that require certain types of data, particularly personal or sensitive information, to be stored within their borders. Organizations that store or process data in cloud environments must be aware of these restrictions and ensure that they comply with local data sovereignty laws. For instance, a company operating in the EU may need to ensure that it stores EU customer data within the EU or in a jurisdiction that has equivalent data protection laws, as per GDPR's data transfer rules.

Compliance with these regulations requires organizations to implement a comprehensive security framework across their IT infrastructure. This includes deploying encryption technologies to protect data, implementing strict access controls to ensure that only authorized personnel can access sensitive information, and using multi-factor authentication (MFA) to strengthen user access security. Additionally, businesses must have mechanisms in place to monitor and audit their IT systems regularly to ensure that compliance standards are being met continuously. Regular security assessments, vulnerability scans, and penetration testing are essential to identify and address potential gaps in security that could lead to non-compliance.

Beyond security, organizations must also ensure that their data management practices comply with applicable regulatory requirements. This includes implementing data retention policies that define how long data should be stored and when it should be deleted. For example, GDPR requires organizations to retain personal data only for as long as necessary to fulfill the purpose for which it was collected. Once the data is no longer required, it must be securely deleted. Data management policies should also include provisions for data accuracy, ensuring that personal data is kept up-to-date and that individuals have the right to correct inaccuracies.

Incident response and disaster recovery planning are also integral components of compliance in IT infrastructure. Regulations such as GDPR, HIPAA, and PCI DSS require organizations to have plans in place to respond to security incidents and breaches promptly. This includes having an incident response team, clear procedures for identifying and containing security breaches, and processes for notifying affected individuals and regulatory authorities. Additionally, organizations must have disaster recovery strategies in place to ensure that they can recover critical data and systems in the event of a natural disaster, cyberattack, or other disruption. Ensuring business continuity is a key element of regulatory compliance, and organizations must be able to demonstrate their ability to recover from incidents swiftly and effectively.

To support compliance efforts, organizations often utilize compliance management tools and audit frameworks. These tools help organizations track their compliance status, generate reports, and ensure that they are adhering to the specific requirements set forth by regulatory bodies. Compliance management platforms often include automated workflows that streamline the process of gathering evidence for audits, reducing the time and effort required to meet compliance deadlines. Moreover, these tools help organizations stay up-to-date with changing regulations by providing alerts and updates on regulatory changes that may affect their operations.

Organizations must also recognize that compliance is not a one-time effort, but an ongoing process that requires continuous monitoring, assessment, and improvement. As new threats emerge and regulations evolve, organizations must stay vigilant and adapt their IT infrastructure to meet the changing compliance landscape. A proactive approach to compliance helps organizations not only avoid penalties but also build trust with customers, partners, and regulators. By prioritizing compliance and integrating regulatory requirements into their IT strategies, businesses can create secure, transparent, and resilient IT infrastructures that support their operations and growth in a rapidly evolving regulatory environment.

Chapter 40: Managing IT Infrastructure Costs and Budgeting

In today's competitive and fast-paced business environment, managing IT infrastructure costs and budgeting effectively is crucial for organizations aiming to stay efficient and innovative while controlling expenses. As IT infrastructure becomes increasingly complex, with the rise of cloud computing, big data, and IoT devices, the financial implications of maintaining and scaling such systems can be significant. Ensuring that IT departments operate within budgetary constraints while providing the necessary resources for business operations requires careful planning, monitoring, and optimization. The process of managing IT infrastructure costs involves a deep understanding of the various components that make up the infrastructure, from hardware and software to network and personnel, and the ability to forecast future needs and align them with organizational goals.

The first step in managing IT infrastructure costs effectively is to gain a clear understanding of the organization's current infrastructure and its associated expenses. This requires an inventory of all IT assets, including servers, storage systems, networking equipment, software licenses, and personnel costs. Organizations must also account for both direct and indirect costs. Direct costs include the purchasing of hardware and software, ongoing subscription fees for cloud services, and the salaries of IT staff responsible for maintaining infrastructure. Indirect costs can be more difficult to quantify but are equally important to consider. These may include the costs of downtime, training, and the opportunity cost of allocating resources to IT management rather than other business initiatives. Understanding the full scope of IT expenses enables businesses to make informed decisions about how to allocate resources and optimize spending.

Once a comprehensive understanding of the current infrastructure costs has been established, the next step is to forecast future needs. Predicting future IT infrastructure requirements can be challenging, as it involves anticipating technological advancements, business growth, and changing market conditions. For example, as a company grows and its operations become more digital, its data storage and processing needs are likely to increase. Similarly, new technologies such as artificial intelligence or machine learning may require additional computing power and specialized infrastructure. Forecasting these needs requires a balance between being proactive and avoiding over-provisioning, which can lead to wasted resources and unnecessary costs.

One of the most effective ways to manage IT infrastructure costs is through the cloud. Cloud computing offers businesses the flexibility to scale their infrastructure according to demand, rather than investing in expensive hardware that may sit idle during periods of low usage. By leveraging cloud services such as Infrastructure as a Service (IaaS) and Platform as a Service (PaaS), companies can rent the computing power, storage, and network resources they need on a pay-as-you-go basis. This model enables businesses to adjust their IT spending based on actual usage, rather than locking themselves into costly long-term commitments. Cloud providers also offer various pricing models, such as reserved instances or spot instances, which can help businesses save money by committing to longer-term usage or taking advantage of unused resources at lower prices.

However, while the cloud offers significant benefits in terms of cost savings and flexibility, organizations must also manage their cloud expenses carefully. One of the common challenges associated with cloud computing is cost creep, where organizations unknowingly accumulate additional costs by failing to monitor usage or optimize their cloud resources. For instance, leaving unused virtual machines or storage volumes active can lead to ongoing charges. To mitigate this risk, businesses should implement robust cloud cost management tools that allow them to track usage, set budgets, and automatically scale down resources during periods of low demand. Regularly reviewing cloud service contracts and usage patterns can help identify opportunities for cost optimization, such as moving to a more cost-effective region or changing service plans to better match the organization's needs.

Another important aspect of managing IT infrastructure costs is optimizing the on-premises infrastructure. While many organizations are shifting to the cloud, on-premises infrastructure still plays a vital role in many IT environments. Managing the costs of on-premises infrastructure involves not only the initial capital expenditure but also the ongoing costs of maintenance, energy consumption, and upgrades. Energy efficiency is a particularly important factor to consider, as data centers and servers can consume significant amounts of power. Investing in energy-efficient hardware, optimizing server utilization, and implementing cooling strategies can help reduce operational costs over time. Additionally, businesses should carefully plan their server lifecycle management, ensuring that hardware is replaced at appropriate intervals and that equipment is properly maintained to avoid expensive repairs or unplanned downtime.

Personnel costs are another significant component of IT infrastructure budgets. As businesses scale their IT operations, the demand for skilled IT professionals also increases. However, staffing IT departments can be costly, especially for small to mid-sized businesses. To manage these costs, organizations can explore alternatives such as outsourcing or leveraging managed services providers (MSPs) to handle specific aspects of IT infrastructure management. For example, businesses can outsource functions such as network monitoring, security, and backup services to specialized vendors, reducing the need for a large in-house IT team. Additionally, adopting automation tools can help reduce the workload on IT staff by streamlining repetitive tasks such as patch management, system monitoring, and resource provisioning.

Optimizing the performance of IT infrastructure is also a critical part of cost management. Performance tuning and capacity planning ensure that resources are allocated efficiently and that systems are running at peak performance without over-provisioning. For example, organizations can use performance monitoring tools to identify bottlenecks in their network or server systems and make adjustments to improve efficiency. Additionally, businesses can implement load balancing and high availability solutions to ensure that resources are distributed efficiently and that systems remain operational during periods of high demand or hardware failure.

A crucial aspect of managing IT infrastructure costs is risk management. Security and compliance requirements are often closely tied to IT infrastructure, and failing to address security risks or regulatory requirements can result in costly fines, reputational damage, and legal issues. Therefore, part of the budgeting process must involve allocating resources for security measures, such as encryption, firewalls, intrusion detection systems, and disaster recovery solutions. These investments help protect the organization's data and systems, minimizing the risk of data breaches and downtime, which can have far-reaching financial consequences.

Finally, effective IT governance is essential for managing IT infrastructure costs. Implementing clear governance policies that define roles, responsibilities, and decision-making processes can help ensure that IT investments align with business goals and that resources are allocated efficiently. IT governance frameworks, such as COBIT or

ITIL, provide structured approaches to managing IT resources and optimizing costs. These frameworks help organizations assess the value of their IT infrastructure investments and ensure that they are delivering the desired outcomes in terms of performance, security, and cost efficiency.

Managing IT infrastructure costs and budgeting is a multifaceted process that requires careful planning, ongoing monitoring, and the strategic use of technology to optimize resources. By understanding the full scope of their IT infrastructure expenses, forecasting future needs, and leveraging cloud services and automation, organizations can ensure that they maintain a balanced approach to cost management. Through effective optimization and risk management, businesses can achieve a more efficient and sustainable IT infrastructure that supports their growth and innovation while minimizing unnecessary costs.

Chapter 41: Virtual Private Networks (VPNs) and Their Uses

Virtual Private Networks (VPNs) have become an essential tool in modern IT infrastructure, offering a secure way for individuals and organizations to access networks and transmit data over the internet. With the increasing reliance on remote work, cloud-based applications, and the expansion of cyber threats, VPNs provide a critical layer of security and privacy. They enable users to connect to private networks securely, regardless of their physical location, and ensure that sensitive data is encrypted and protected from unauthorized access. The versatility and widespread adoption of VPNs have made them an indispensable part of both corporate and personal cybersecurity strategies.

A VPN is essentially a technology that creates a secure, encrypted tunnel between a user's device and a remote server, often located within a private network. When connected to a VPN, all data that is sent or received by the user is routed through this encrypted tunnel, making it difficult for external parties to intercept or tamper with the data. This encryption ensures that even if the data passes through unsecured public networks, such as those found in cafes, airports, or public Wi-Fi hotspots, it remains protected. By hiding the user's actual IP address and routing traffic through a VPN server, VPNs also help maintain privacy and anonymity online.

One of the primary uses of VPNs is to enhance security when accessing the internet, particularly over untrusted or insecure networks. Public Wi-Fi networks, while convenient, are often vulnerable to attacks, such as eavesdropping or man-in-the-middle attacks, where malicious actors intercept communication between the user and the destination server. VPNs mitigate these risks by ensuring that all transmitted data is encrypted, rendering it unreadable to anyone attempting to intercept it. This makes VPNs a critical tool for users who frequently access the internet from public locations, where network security cannot be guaranteed.

For businesses, VPNs are crucial for enabling secure remote access to internal company networks. In the past, many employees worked exclusively from corporate offices, and all network traffic was routed through the organization's internal infrastructure. However, with the rise of remote work, employees need secure access to company resources, including file servers, internal websites, and databases, regardless of their location. A VPN allows remote employees to securely connect to the company's private network, as if they were physically present at the office. This capability is especially important for businesses with a distributed workforce or for those that allow employees to work from home or while traveling.

VPNs also play an important role in protecting sensitive data. Many organizations deal with confidential information that needs to be kept secure, such as financial data, personal customer information, and intellectual property. By encrypting data during transmission, VPNs help ensure that this information is not exposed to unauthorized individuals, reducing the risk of data breaches or leaks. This is especially critical for industries that are subject to regulatory requirements, such as healthcare and finance, where non-compliance with data protection laws can result in significant penalties and reputational damage.

Another significant use of VPNs is in bypassing geographic restrictions and accessing region-locked content. Many online services, such as video streaming platforms and websites, restrict access to certain content based on the user's geographic location. For example, a streaming service may offer different content libraries in the United States and the United Kingdom, or some services may be unavailable in certain countries altogether. By using a VPN, users can connect to a server in a different location, effectively masking their real IP address and making it appear as if they are accessing the internet from that region. This allows them to access content that would otherwise be unavailable to them.

For businesses operating in multiple countries or regions, VPNs also help establish secure site-to-site connections between geographically dispersed offices. These connections allow different offices to securely share data, applications, and resources, as if they were part of the same local network. Site-to-site VPNs are often used by multinational companies that need to securely connect remote branches or data centers to the central office network. This provides a consistent and secure method of communication between different locations, ensuring that data is protected while in transit.

In addition to enhancing security and privacy, VPNs also contribute to network performance in some cases. By using VPNs to route traffic through specific servers, organizations can manage network traffic more effectively, ensuring that critical data gets priority over less important traffic. VPNs can also be used to route traffic around bottlenecks, allowing users to avoid congested or unreliable networks. For example, an organization operating in a region with unreliable internet access might use a VPN to connect to a server in a more stable location, improving overall network performance.

Despite their numerous benefits, VPNs are not without challenges. One of the primary issues with VPNs is their impact on performance. Encrypting and decrypting data requires processing power, which can lead to latency and slower connection speeds, especially if the VPN server is located far from the user or if the encryption methods used are particularly resource-intensive. This can be problematic for users who need high-speed access to data or for applications that require low-latency communication, such as video conferencing or online gaming. To address these issues, many organizations choose to use split tunneling, a configuration that allows users to access some resources through the VPN while accessing other resources directly through their local network. This reduces the load on the VPN server and improves performance for non-sensitive activities.

Another challenge with VPNs is ensuring proper configuration and management. VPNs require careful setup to ensure that they are both secure and functional. For example, improper configuration of VPN settings can lead to vulnerabilities, such as unsecured traffic or the potential for DNS leaks, where users' internet activity is exposed. Additionally, organizations need to manage VPN user access carefully, ensuring that only authorized users can access the corporate network. Failure to implement strong authentication methods or to monitor and manage VPN connections can lead to unauthorized access or misuse of sensitive information.

The advent of next-generation VPN technologies has helped address some of these challenges. Technologies like SSL/TLS VPNs and IPsec VPNs provide more secure and flexible alternatives to traditional VPN protocols. These newer technologies offer improved encryption, better support for mobile devices, and stronger security measures. Furthermore, with the rise of cloud services and mobile workforces, VPN providers have developed more scalable and efficient solutions that allow users to connect securely to cloud applications and resources from anywhere.

For businesses, choosing the right VPN solution requires balancing security, performance, and cost. While VPNs are essential for protecting data and ensuring secure remote access, they can be resource-intensive and costly to implement and maintain. Organizations must carefully evaluate their security needs, the size and structure of their workforce, and their budget constraints when selecting a VPN solution. A well-chosen VPN solution can significantly enhance security, privacy, and operational efficiency, but it requires proper planning and management to realize its full potential.

As remote work and cloud services continue to expand, the role of VPNs in IT infrastructure will only grow. By providing secure, encrypted connections for users, enabling secure access to cloud resources, and protecting sensitive data, VPNs will remain a fundamental technology in the cybersecurity landscape. With continuous advancements in VPN technologies, businesses can expect even more powerful and flexible solutions to meet their evolving needs in an increasingly digital world.

Chapter 42: Disaster Recovery Planning and Business Continuity

Disaster recovery planning and business continuity are critical components of any organization's risk management strategy, ensuring that IT infrastructure, data, and operations can withstand unexpected disruptions and continue functioning even in the face of major incidents. The modern business landscape is increasingly dependent on technology, making it more vulnerable to threats such as cyberattacks, natural disasters, equipment failures, and other unforeseen events that can bring operations to a halt. As such, having a well-defined disaster recovery plan (DRP) and business continuity plan (BCP) in place is essential for minimizing downtime, protecting valuable data, and maintaining critical services in the face of adversity.

Disaster recovery planning focuses on the processes and procedures that organizations must follow to restore IT infrastructure, applications, and data in the event of a disaster. The goal of a disaster recovery plan is to ensure that systems can be recovered as quickly as possible, minimizing the impact on business operations. A DRP typically includes detailed steps for backing up data, recovering critical systems, and restoring access to applications and services. It also addresses issues such as data integrity, system dependencies, and the resources required to bring systems back online. The scope of a disaster recovery plan can vary depending on the size of the organization and the complexity of its IT infrastructure, but its primary goal is always to provide a clear and organized approach to recovery.

Business continuity, on the other hand, is a broader concept that encompasses the overall ability of an organization to continue operating in the event of a disruption. While disaster recovery is primarily concerned with IT systems and data, business continuity involves ensuring that all aspects of the organization—such as personnel, communications, supply chains, and customer relationships—can continue functioning even during a crisis. A business continuity plan (BCP) includes strategies for maintaining essential business functions, protecting critical infrastructure, and ensuring that employees are able to carry out their duties despite disruptions. The BCP should be closely aligned with the DRP to ensure that recovery efforts are integrated with broader organizational goals and that the organization as a whole can remain operational during an emergency.

An essential aspect of both disaster recovery and business continuity planning is risk assessment. Organizations must identify the potential risks that could disrupt their operations and assess the impact of these risks on various aspects of the business. This involves considering both natural disasters, such as earthquakes, floods, or fires, as well as man-made threats, such as cyberattacks, system failures, and supply chain disruptions. Understanding the likelihood and potential impact of each threat allows businesses to prioritize their recovery efforts and allocate resources effectively. For example, a financial institution may prioritize the recovery of its transaction processing systems due to their critical role in customer operations, while a manufacturing company may focus on ensuring the continuity of its production lines.

Once risks have been identified and assessed, the next step is to define recovery objectives. Recovery objectives are critical metrics that help guide the disaster recovery and business continuity efforts. These include the Recovery Time Objective (RTO) and Recovery Point Objective (RPO). The RTO defines the maximum acceptable amount of time that a system, application, or process can be down before it severely impacts the business. The RPO, on the other hand, refers to the maximum amount of data loss that is acceptable in the event of a disaster. These objectives help organizations determine the resources and strategies required to meet their recovery goals, ensuring that the business can continue operating effectively after a disruption.

Data backup and redundancy are fundamental components of any disaster recovery plan. Regular backups are essential for protecting data from loss due to hardware failures, human errors, or malicious attacks. Organizations should implement a robust backup strategy that includes both onsite and offsite backups, ensuring that copies of critical data are stored in different physical locations. Cloud-based backups are increasingly popular, as they provide a secure and scalable solution for storing data offsite. In addition to regular backups, organizations should implement data redundancy mechanisms to ensure that critical systems can continue to function even if one component fails. Redundant systems, such as failover clusters or load balancing, allow organizations to maintain service availability during outages by redirecting traffic to backup systems.

Testing and validation of disaster recovery plans are crucial for ensuring that they will work as intended when needed. A DRP is only as effective as the preparation and testing behind it. Regular testing of the disaster recovery procedures allows organizations to identify gaps or weaknesses in their plans and make necessary improvements before a real disaster occurs. Testing should simulate a range of potential disaster scenarios, from simple server failures to complex cybersecurity incidents. These tests should involve all relevant stakeholders, including IT personnel, business units, and third-party vendors, to ensure that everyone understands their role in the recovery process and can respond effectively under pressure.

In addition to technical recovery measures, business continuity plans should address employee preparedness. In the event of a disaster, employees must be able to continue performing their duties, either from a remote location or through alternate work arrangements. Businesses should establish clear communication protocols to ensure that employees are informed about the status of the disaster and the steps they need to take to continue their work. Remote work policies and tools, such as virtual private networks (VPNs) and collaboration platforms, are essential for enabling employees to work from home or other locations during a disruption. Training programs that teach employees how to respond to emergencies and use remote tools effectively are an important part of business continuity planning.

Another critical aspect of disaster recovery and business continuity is ensuring that third-party vendors and partners are included in the planning process. Many businesses rely on external suppliers, cloud providers, and service providers to support their operations. It is essential to assess the business continuity capabilities of these third-party vendors and ensure that their recovery plans align with the organization's needs. Organizations should establish clear expectations for service availability and recovery in their contracts with vendors and ensure that these vendors can meet the same recovery objectives as the business itself. This can be done through regular reviews of vendor continuity plans, performance monitoring, and testing.

Lastly, disaster recovery and business continuity plans should be continually updated to reflect changes in the organization's IT infrastructure, business operations, and external environment. As technology evolves, new risks emerge, and business processes change, so too should the plans that safeguard an organization's operations. A proactive approach to updating and improving disaster recovery and business continuity strategies ensures that businesses remain prepared for any eventuality and can recover swiftly in the face of adversity.

Developing and maintaining comprehensive disaster recovery and business continuity plans is vital for the resilience of any organization. By understanding potential risks, defining recovery objectives, and implementing robust recovery strategies, organizations can ensure that they are well-equipped to handle disruptions and continue their operations with minimal downtime. This preparedness not only safeguards critical data and IT infrastructure but also helps organizations maintain trust with customers, partners, and stakeholders, reinforcing their long-term success and stability.

Chapter 43: Remote Management of IT Infrastructure

Remote management of IT infrastructure has become a fundamental aspect of modern IT operations, offering businesses the flexibility to monitor, configure, and maintain their systems from anywhere in the world. As organizations increasingly adopt cloud computing, remote work models, and distributed IT environments, the need for efficient remote management solutions has grown. The ability to remotely manage IT infrastructure ensures that IT teams can quickly address issues, ensure systems remain operational, and scale resources as needed, all without being physically present in the data center or office. This level of flexibility has transformed how IT departments operate and has become a key enabler for business continuity, particularly in a world where teams are dispersed and access to on-premises infrastructure may be limited or impractical.

The concept of remote management encompasses a variety of activities, from monitoring the performance of servers, networks, and storage systems to configuring and troubleshooting hardware and software remotely. For many organizations, the need for remote management arose as a response to the growing complexity of IT environments. With the proliferation of cloud services, hybrid infrastructure, and an increasing number of endpoints, managing IT infrastructure using traditional, hands-on methods became increasingly difficult. Remote management allows IT administrators to take control of infrastructure systems from any location, often through web-based management interfaces, VPNs, or remote desktop protocols, without the need to be physically on-site.

A key benefit of remote management is efficiency. IT administrators are often responsible for large, complex environments, including servers, network devices, storage systems, and security infrastructure. Remote management tools allow them to access these systems quickly and troubleshoot or configure them without having to travel to data centers or individual offices. This can be particularly useful for organizations with geographically dispersed offices or remote data centers. With remote access, IT staff can address issues promptly, reducing downtime and ensuring that business operations continue smoothly.

Moreover, scalability is another critical advantage of remote management. As organizations grow, so does the need to manage increasingly complex IT environments. Whether it involves adding new servers to the network, deploying software updates, or managing cloud-based services, remote management enables IT departments to scale operations without needing to increase on-site personnel. Remote management solutions allow administrators to automate routine tasks, such as system updates and patch management, which can be done in the background, freeing up IT staff to focus on higher-priority tasks. Automated monitoring and reporting tools can also provide real-time alerts about system performance or potential security breaches, enabling quick responses to prevent larger issues.

Remote management solutions are especially important in the context of business continuity. In a globalized business environment, IT teams may not always be physically present to manage infrastructure, especially in cases of natural disasters, remote work situations, or during international expansion. By adopting remote management systems, organizations can ensure that their IT infrastructure remains operational regardless of geographic location or external circumstances. During crises or disasters, IT staff can access and restore critical systems remotely, ensuring business continuity with minimal disruption. Cloud-based services and remote management solutions, such as remote desktop tools or web-based dashboards, allow IT teams to quickly recover data, address system failures, or deploy temporary fixes without needing to be on-site.

The security of remote management is a significant concern, as it often involves accessing critical systems over the internet. Securing these remote connections is paramount, as unauthorized access to systems could result in data breaches, system compromise, or operational disruptions. To mitigate these risks, remote management tools incorporate robust security measures, including encryption, multi-factor authentication (MFA), and secure tunneling protocols, such as Virtual Private Networks (VPNs). These measures ensure that only authorized personnel can access sensitive systems and that all communication is encrypted to prevent interception. Regular security audits, as well as monitoring and logging of remote access activities, help detect and respond to any suspicious behavior, maintaining the integrity of the infrastructure.

One of the challenges of remote management is the integration of disparate systems and technologies. Many organizations rely on a mix of on-premises infrastructure, private and public clouds, and third-party services, all of which may require different tools and platforms for remote management. Ensuring that these various systems can be effectively managed from a central location requires the use of comprehensive, integrated management platforms. These platforms provide a unified interface that consolidates access to different infrastructure components, allowing IT administrators to monitor performance, configure settings, and deploy updates across the entire network. Integration tools and APIs also facilitate the synchronization of different systems, ensuring that remote management capabilities are seamlessly extended to all aspects of the IT infrastructure.

Cost-effectiveness is another key driver of remote management adoption. Traveling to physical locations to manage IT infrastructure or hiring on-site personnel to monitor systems can be costly and inefficient. Remote management reduces the need for physical presence, allowing IT teams to manage multiple systems across different locations from a central hub. This not only saves time and travel expenses but also optimizes the use of IT resources. Organizations can invest in fewer on-site technicians and instead rely on skilled professionals who can remotely manage and support a wider array of systems. Additionally, many remote management tools are available as subscription-based services, making them more affordable for organizations that may not have the resources for large-scale infrastructure management.

The flexibility provided by remote management is also invaluable in today's business landscape. As more businesses adopt hybrid and multi-cloud environments, IT infrastructure becomes increasingly decentralized. Remote management tools allow businesses to control their infrastructure no matter where it resides—whether on local servers, within a private cloud, or hosted on a public cloud platform. This centralized control enables IT teams to streamline their operations and provides the flexibility to adapt to new technologies or business requirements quickly. For instance, businesses can scale their cloud infrastructure up or down without needing to deploy physical hardware, all while maintaining control and visibility from a remote management platform.

Another important aspect of remote management is monitoring and troubleshooting. Real-time monitoring tools allow IT teams to track the health of infrastructure systems, identifying potential issues before they escalate into critical failures. These tools can be configured to send alerts or automatically trigger corrective actions when certain thresholds are met, such as high CPU usage, network congestion, or low disk space. Remote management platforms often include diagnostic tools that enable administrators to troubleshoot and resolve issues without needing to access physical hardware. This speeds up the resolution process and helps ensure that systems remain operational, minimizing the impact on business activities.

Collaboration and collaboration tools play a significant role in enhancing the efficiency of remote management. IT teams can work together in real time, regardless of location, to resolve issues, deploy changes, or manage complex configurations. Shared dashboards, cloud-based documentation, and communication platforms enable teams to collaborate effectively, ensuring that everyone involved is on the same page. This fosters a more cohesive, responsive IT department that can respond to challenges quickly and efficiently, even when team members are distributed across different regions.

Remote management of IT infrastructure is an essential practice for modern businesses seeking to optimize their operations, improve efficiency, and enhance security. It enables IT teams to monitor, manage, and troubleshoot systems from anywhere, providing flexibility and scalability without the need for a physical presence. By leveraging the right tools, organizations can ensure that their IT infrastructure remains secure, functional, and adaptable in an increasingly digital world. Through the careful implementation of remote management solutions, businesses can enhance their operational resilience and continue to innovate and grow in a rapidly evolving technological landscape.

Chapter 44: Managing IT Infrastructure in the Cloud

The management of IT infrastructure in the cloud has become one of the most transformative developments in the field of information technology. Cloud computing offers businesses a powerful model for accessing and managing computing resources, such as storage, processing power, and networking, without the need to invest in expensive physical hardware. This flexibility and scalability have made cloud computing the backbone of modern IT infrastructure for organizations of all sizes. Managing IT infrastructure in the cloud, however, requires a shift in how IT teams approach infrastructure provisioning, security, resource allocation, and cost management. As organizations continue to embrace cloud services, understanding the intricacies of cloud infrastructure management has become a vital skill for IT professionals.

Cloud computing can be broadly categorized into three main models: Infrastructure as a Service (IaaS), Platform as a Service (PaaS), and Software as a Service (SaaS). IaaS provides the most direct access to cloud resources, allowing businesses to rent virtualized computing resources, including servers, storage, and networking. PaaS, on the other hand, offers a more abstracted platform where developers can build and deploy applications without managing the underlying hardware and operating systems. SaaS delivers fully managed software applications over the cloud, removing the need for organizations to install, manage, or maintain their own software. Each of these models provides different levels of control and responsibility, but all rely on cloud infrastructure providers to deliver and maintain the physical resources that underpin the services.

One of the most significant advantages of cloud computing is scalability. With traditional on-premises infrastructure, businesses must anticipate their resource needs and invest in hardware that can accommodate peak demand. This often results in over-provisioning, where businesses purchase more hardware than necessary to ensure they can meet future demand. The cloud eliminates this problem by offering on-demand access to computing resources, which can be scaled up or down based on real-time usage. This flexibility allows businesses to align their infrastructure resources with their actual needs, optimizing both performance and cost efficiency. For example, an e-commerce website may experience a surge in traffic during the holiday season, and with cloud infrastructure, it can quickly scale its resources to accommodate the increased demand, only paying for the resources used during that period.

However, managing cloud infrastructure also requires effective resource allocation. With the ability to scale on-demand, it is easy to quickly provision cloud resources, but this flexibility can lead to inefficiencies and increased costs if not carefully managed. Organizations must monitor usage and performance metrics to ensure they are optimizing their resource allocation and avoiding unnecessary expenditure. Cloud providers offer a variety of tools for resource management, such as automated scaling, load balancing, and resource usage tracking, which help organizations fine-tune their infrastructure to balance performance with cost. Additionally, businesses must carefully consider the specific cloud services and pricing models offered by their provider to ensure they are selecting the most appropriate options for their needs.

One of the challenges of managing IT infrastructure in the cloud is maintaining security. While cloud providers invest heavily in securing their physical infrastructure, businesses must take responsibility for securing their data and applications within the cloud. This includes implementing strong access controls, ensuring data encryption both at rest and in transit, and configuring firewalls and security groups to protect cloud resources from unauthorized access. The shared responsibility model in cloud security means that the cloud provider is responsible for securing the underlying infrastructure, but businesses must secure their data, applications, and user access. As organizations store more sensitive data in the cloud, they must implement comprehensive security policies and regularly audit their cloud environments for vulnerabilities.

Another important aspect of cloud infrastructure management is data management. As organizations migrate to the cloud, they must establish clear policies and strategies for managing their data. This includes determining what data to store in the cloud, how to back it up, and how to ensure it is properly organized and protected. Cloud environments often provide automated data management tools, such as backups, disaster recovery, and version control, which help organizations manage and protect their data. Additionally, organizations must consider data sovereignty issues, particularly if they operate in multiple regions or countries. Many cloud providers offer geographically distributed data centers, but businesses must ensure they comply with local data protection laws and regulations, such as the General Data Protection Regulation (GDPR) in the EU, when storing data in the cloud.

In cloud environments, monitoring and performance management are crucial for ensuring the health and efficiency of IT infrastructure. Cloud providers offer a wide range of monitoring tools that allow businesses to track the performance of their cloud resources in real time. These tools provide valuable insights into the utilization of compute resources, network traffic, storage capacity, and application performance. By continuously monitoring cloud infrastructure, businesses can identify potential issues before they affect operations, such as bottlenecks or system failures, and can take corrective actions to maintain optimal performance. Additionally, performance metrics can be used to help businesses make data-driven decisions about scaling their infrastructure or optimizing their applications.

Cost management is another essential aspect of managing IT infrastructure in the cloud. While the cloud offers many financial benefits, such as the ability to pay only for the resources used, organizations can quickly accumulate high costs if they do not carefully manage their cloud spending. Cloud providers offer various pricing models, such as pay-as-you-go, reserved instances, and spot instances, each with different cost implications. Businesses must understand these models and select the most cost-effective options for their usage patterns. Additionally, cloud cost management tools can help businesses monitor their spending, set budgets, and track resource utilization. By leveraging these tools, businesses can gain better visibility into their cloud expenses and ensure they are staying within budget.

As organizations become more reliant on cloud infrastructure, multi-cloud and hybrid cloud strategies are also gaining popularity. A multi-cloud strategy involves using multiple cloud providers to distribute workloads and reduce dependency on a single vendor, while a hybrid cloud approach integrates on-premises infrastructure with cloud resources. These strategies offer greater flexibility, redundancy, and resilience, as businesses can leverage the strengths of different providers and avoid potential risks associated with vendor lock-in. However, managing multi-cloud and hybrid cloud environments introduces additional complexity, as organizations must integrate different cloud platforms, ensure consistent security policies across environments, and optimize resource allocation across multiple cloud providers.

Cloud infrastructure management also involves ongoing compliance and regulatory adherence. As cloud adoption increases, organizations must ensure that their cloud environments comply with industry regulations and standards. Many industries, such as healthcare, finance, and government, have strict data protection and privacy laws that require organizations to store and process data in specific ways. Cloud providers often offer compliance certifications and tools to help businesses meet these requirements, but it remains the responsibility of the organization to implement appropriate controls and procedures within their cloud environments. Regular audits, security assessments, and vulnerability scans are essential for maintaining compliance in the cloud.

Managing IT infrastructure in the cloud requires a shift in how businesses approach their technology environments. While cloud computing offers significant advantages in terms of scalability, flexibility, and cost savings, it also introduces challenges related to security, resource management, data sovereignty, and compliance. Effective cloud infrastructure management requires a proactive approach, leveraging the right tools and strategies to optimize performance, maintain security, and control costs. As businesses continue to move more of their operations to the cloud, understanding the nuances of cloud infrastructure management will be essential for maximizing the benefits of this transformative technology.

Chapter 45: The Role of DevOps in IT Infrastructure Management

DevOps has become a transformative approach to IT infrastructure management, bridging the gap between development and operations teams to improve collaboration, automation, and efficiency in software delivery. The traditional separation between development and operations often led to silos within an organization, with each team working in isolation on their own respective tasks. This resulted in slower release cycles, poor communication, and often a lack of alignment between development and IT operations. DevOps has emerged as a solution to these issues by fostering a culture of collaboration, shared responsibility, and continuous improvement, allowing businesses to respond faster to market demands while ensuring that infrastructure remains stable and reliable.

At its core, DevOps integrates software development (Dev) and IT operations (Ops) through practices that focus on automation, monitoring, testing, and collaboration. DevOps enables IT teams to automate repetitive tasks such as code deployment, system provisioning, and configuration management, freeing up time for more strategic activities. This automation not only accelerates workflows but also reduces the potential for human error, which can be costly in complex IT environments. By automating processes, DevOps helps ensure consistency across environments, reducing configuration drift and making it easier to manage infrastructure at scale.

One of the primary benefits of DevOps in IT infrastructure management is continuous integration and continuous delivery (CI/CD). CI/CD pipelines are at the heart of DevOps practices and play a crucial role in automating the development and deployment of applications. Continuous integration refers to the practice of frequently merging code changes into a central repository, where automated tests are run to verify the quality and functionality of the code. Continuous delivery builds on this by automating the deployment process, ensuring that code can be reliably released to production with minimal manual intervention. This reduces the time between writing code and delivering it to users, enabling businesses to deliver new features, updates, and fixes faster. The rapid feedback loop provided by CI/CD pipelines ensures that developers can quickly identify and resolve issues before they escalate into production problems.

In the context of IT infrastructure, DevOps plays a vital role in improving infrastructure as code (IaC). Infrastructure as code allows IT teams to manage and provision infrastructure using code and automated scripts, rather than manually configuring hardware or systems. IaC makes it possible to define infrastructure configurations in a consistent, repeatable manner, which significantly improves the efficiency and reliability of infrastructure management. Through IaC, DevOps teams can automate the provisioning of servers, networks, and storage, and can also ensure that infrastructure is configured correctly across different environments. This also enables teams to rapidly scale their infrastructure, as code can be reused and adapted to create new environments without the need for manual intervention.

A key aspect of DevOps is the use of collaboration and communication tools, which help facilitate better interaction between development and operations teams. Tools such as Slack, Jira, GitHub, and GitLab allow teams to coordinate efforts in real-time, share feedback, and track the progress of tasks. These tools enhance transparency across departments, enabling both developers and IT operations teams to stay aligned on project goals and timelines. By fostering a culture of communication, DevOps breaks down traditional barriers between teams and encourages a more holistic approach to managing IT infrastructure.

Another significant role of DevOps in IT infrastructure management is its focus on monitoring and performance. Continuous monitoring is an essential part of the DevOps lifecycle, as it provides teams with real-time insights into the health and performance of applications and infrastructure. This allows teams to quickly identify issues, such as performance bottlenecks, system failures, or security vulnerabilities, and respond to them before they affect users or the business. Monitoring tools, such as Prometheus, Grafana, and Nagios, help teams visualize system performance and metrics, enabling proactive management of infrastructure. Additionally, by integrating monitoring with automated response systems, DevOps teams can create self-healing infrastructure that can automatically address certain types of failures, reducing the need for manual intervention and improving system reliability.

DevOps also contributes to scalability in IT infrastructure management. As businesses grow, so do their IT infrastructure needs. Scaling infrastructure manually can be a time-consuming and error-prone process, but DevOps practices help to automate and streamline scaling. Through IaC and automation tools, DevOps teams can quickly provision and de-provision resources to meet changing demand. For example, in a cloud environment, DevOps practices can automatically scale compute resources based on load, ensuring that infrastructure can handle peak traffic without over-provisioning or underutilizing resources. This scalability is especially important in modern cloud-based architectures, where businesses may experience fluctuating workloads and need the flexibility to scale efficiently.

Security is another area where DevOps plays a crucial role. Traditionally, security was often treated as a separate concern handled by dedicated security teams after the development process. However, DevOps encourages a more integrated approach to security, often referred to as DevSecOps. In this approach, security is embedded into every stage of the DevOps pipeline, from the initial design phase to continuous monitoring and deployment. This means that vulnerabilities are identified and addressed earlier in the development cycle, rather than being patched after the fact. Automated security testing, such as static code analysis and vulnerability scanning, can be incorporated into CI/CD pipelines, ensuring that security issues are addressed before code is deployed to production.

The role of DevOps extends to cost optimization in IT infrastructure as well. By automating repetitive tasks, improving resource allocation, and enabling more efficient scaling, DevOps can help businesses reduce infrastructure-related costs. In a cloud environment, for example, DevOps teams can automatically scale resources up or down based on demand, ensuring that businesses only pay for the resources they actually need. Automation also reduces the need for manual intervention, cutting down on labor costs and reducing the risk of errors that could lead to costly downtime or system failures. Furthermore, DevOps can help optimize the use of cloud resources, preventing waste and ensuring that IT teams make the most efficient use of their infrastructure.

Another important aspect of DevOps is its emphasis on continuous improvement. DevOps is built on the principle of continuous feedback and iteration, meaning that infrastructure management practices are constantly evolving to meet the changing needs of the business. After each deployment, teams gather feedback on system performance, user experience, and operational efficiency, and use this feedback to make improvements. This iterative approach allows organizations to quickly adapt to new challenges and continuously enhance their IT infrastructure to keep up with technological advancements and business requirements.

DevOps is not just a set of tools or practices, but a cultural shift in how IT teams approach infrastructure management. By promoting collaboration, automation, and continuous improvement, DevOps enables organizations to deliver high-quality applications and services faster, while maintaining the reliability and security of their IT infrastructure. The adoption of DevOps practices has become essential for businesses looking to stay competitive in an increasingly fast-paced, technology-driven world. Through the seamless integration of development and operations, DevOps helps organizations optimize their IT infrastructure, improve performance, and drive innovation.

Chapter 46: Automation and Orchestration in IT Infrastructure

In the rapidly evolving landscape of IT infrastructure, automation and orchestration have become integral to managing and optimizing systems. The complexities of modern IT environments, which often span on-premises data centers, cloud platforms, and hybrid infrastructures, require new approaches to streamline operations, improve efficiency, and reduce human error. Automation and orchestration help organizations manage their infrastructure more effectively by automating repetitive tasks and ensuring that various systems and services work together seamlessly. These technologies play a pivotal role in enhancing the speed, reliability, and scalability of IT operations, allowing businesses to focus on innovation rather than on the manual aspects of infrastructure management.

Automation in IT infrastructure refers to the use of software tools and scripts to automate repetitive tasks that were traditionally performed manually by IT staff. These tasks can range from simple processes, such as system monitoring and patch management, to more complex activities, such as software deployment, configuration, and network management. The primary goal of automation is to reduce the amount of manual intervention required for infrastructure management, thereby improving operational efficiency, reducing errors, and freeing up IT staff to focus on more strategic initiatives. By automating routine processes, businesses can ensure that tasks are performed consistently and at scale, which is especially important in large, dynamic environments where the complexity of managing systems grows exponentially.

One of the core benefits of automation is its ability to improve the speed and efficiency of IT operations. With manual processes, tasks can take a considerable amount of time and effort, and the potential for human error increases with the complexity of the environment. Automation removes much of this burden by executing tasks according to predefined rules, reducing the time it takes to complete repetitive processes and ensuring that they are performed without error. For example, automating the patching process can ensure that critical updates are applied across all systems in a timely manner, without the risk of oversight or inconsistency. Similarly, automating the provisioning of resources, such as virtual machines or storage, can significantly speed up the deployment process, enabling businesses to scale their infrastructure rapidly in response to changing demands.

Alongside automation, orchestration is another key concept that plays an essential role in modern IT infrastructure management. While automation focuses on the execution of specific tasks, orchestration involves the coordination of multiple tasks and processes across different systems and environments to achieve a desired outcome. Orchestration allows organizations to manage complex workflows that involve multiple systems, applications, and services, ensuring that they interact with one another in a seamless and efficient manner. For example, in a cloud environment, orchestration can be used to automatically provision resources, configure networks, and deploy applications based on predefined rules. By automating these workflows, orchestration ensures that all components work together harmoniously and that business processes run smoothly.

The combination of automation and orchestration is particularly valuable in cloud environments and hybrid infrastructures, where resources are often distributed across multiple locations. As businesses increasingly migrate to the cloud and adopt hybrid IT models, managing infrastructure becomes more complex, requiring the coordination of various cloud providers, on-premises resources, and third-party services. Orchestration platforms, such as Kubernetes for container orchestration or tools like Ansible and Terraform for infrastructure automation, allow organizations to manage this complexity by providing a unified platform to define, deploy, and monitor infrastructure and services. These platforms ensure that the necessary resources are available, configured correctly, and integrated with other systems, providing businesses with the flexibility and agility needed to support modern applications and workflows.

One of the major advantages of automation and orchestration is scalability. In the past, scaling infrastructure involved manually adding new servers, configuring networks, and updating software configurations, which was time-consuming and error-prone. With automation and orchestration, scaling becomes a much more efficient and streamlined process. For example, cloud-based services like Amazon Web Services (AWS), Microsoft Azure, and Google Cloud offer built-in automation tools that can automatically scale resources up or down based on demand. This allows businesses to dynamically adjust their infrastructure to meet changing requirements, without the need for manual intervention. The ability to scale infrastructure quickly and efficiently is especially important for businesses with fluctuating workloads or those that experience rapid growth, as it ensures that resources are always available to meet demand without over-provisioning or underutilizing resources.

Cost optimization is another key benefit of automation and orchestration in IT infrastructure. By automating the provisioning and management of resources, businesses can reduce the time and effort required to manage their infrastructure, leading to cost savings. Automation also helps prevent over-provisioning, ensuring that resources are only used when needed, which helps control costs in cloud environments where businesses are billed based on usage. Orchestration tools can also help organizations optimize resource utilization by automatically allocating resources based on workload demand, ensuring that they are using their infrastructure efficiently. This can be particularly valuable in large-scale environments where manual management would be costly and inefficient.

In addition to cost and efficiency benefits, automation and orchestration also improve reliability and consistency. In traditional IT environments, manual processes are often prone to errors and inconsistencies, especially when they involve complex configurations or large-scale infrastructure. Automation ensures that tasks are performed consistently across all systems, reducing the risk of configuration drift and ensuring that all systems are set up in accordance with predefined policies. Orchestration ensures that tasks are executed in the correct sequence and that dependencies between systems are managed effectively, preventing errors that could arise from improper configurations or incomplete processes. This increased consistency leads to more reliable infrastructure, which is essential for maintaining uptime and minimizing disruptions to business operations.

Another important aspect of automation and orchestration is security. As businesses face increasing security threats, automation can help enforce security policies consistently across all systems, ensuring that security updates are applied promptly, access controls are enforced, and compliance requirements are met. Automated security tools can scan systems for vulnerabilities, monitor network traffic for suspicious activity, and automatically respond to security incidents in real time. Orchestration platforms can coordinate security measures across multiple systems, ensuring that security protocols are consistently applied across an organization's entire IT infrastructure. By automating security tasks and orchestrating responses, businesses can improve their ability to detect, respond to, and mitigate security threats, reducing the risk of breaches and other security incidents.

While automation and orchestration provide numerous benefits, implementing these technologies requires careful planning and execution. Organizations must ensure that their automation and orchestration tools are compatible with their existing IT infrastructure and that they are configured correctly to meet their specific needs. Additionally, businesses must invest in training their IT teams to understand the complexities of automation and orchestration, as these technologies require new skills and expertise. Furthermore, ongoing monitoring and maintenance are required to ensure that automated processes continue to function as expected and that orchestration workflows remain efficient as the infrastructure evolves.

Automation and orchestration are indispensable components of modern IT infrastructure management, enabling businesses to achieve greater efficiency, scalability, and reliability. By automating routine tasks, orchestrating complex workflows, and optimizing resource usage, organizations can streamline their operations, reduce costs, and improve service delivery. As businesses continue to adopt cloud technologies and increasingly complex IT environments, automation and orchestration will play an even greater role in ensuring that infrastructure remains agile, secure, and aligned with business goals. Through the intelligent use of these technologies, organizations can transform their IT operations and drive greater value from their infrastructure investments.

Chapter 47: Managing IT Assets and Inventory

Effective management of IT assets and inventory is essential for organizations to optimize their technology investments and maintain operational efficiency. IT assets, including hardware, software, and network equipment, are critical components of an organization's infrastructure, and managing them properly ensures that these resources are used to their full potential. Whether a company is managing on-premises servers, workstations, cloud resources, or licensed software, having a structured approach to asset and inventory management is key to minimizing costs, reducing risks, and ensuring that IT systems function smoothly. As organizations become more reliant on complex IT environments, the need for effective asset management and inventory control has grown, especially given the rapid pace of technological change and the increasing complexity of IT infrastructures.

IT asset management (ITAM) involves the process of tracking and managing the lifecycle of an organization's technology assets from procurement to disposal. It starts with identifying and documenting all hardware and software assets within the organization. This documentation includes details such as the asset type, manufacturer, model, serial number, purchase date, and warranty status. By keeping an accurate record of these assets, organizations can ensure that they are aware of what they own, how it is used, and when it is due for maintenance or replacement. A well-maintained asset inventory helps businesses track the status of their IT resources, identify gaps or redundancies in the infrastructure, and make informed decisions about future investments.

A significant aspect of IT asset management is lifecycle management. From the moment an asset is acquired, it enters a lifecycle that typically includes stages such as procurement, deployment, maintenance, and ultimately decommissioning or disposal. Throughout each stage of the lifecycle, asset management tools can help organizations track the asset's status and performance. For instance, during the deployment phase, businesses can ensure that assets are properly configured and integrated into the existing infrastructure. Maintenance and support records can be tracked to ensure that hardware is regularly updated or repaired, and software licenses are renewed in time. As assets approach the end of their useful life, businesses can plan for upgrades, replacements, or recycling, ensuring that old hardware and software are properly disposed of, either by selling, recycling, or safely destroying it to protect sensitive data.

A comprehensive inventory management system is the backbone of efficient IT asset management. This system helps organizations catalog their assets and monitor their usage in real time. An inventory management system can also automate the tracking of items such as laptops, desktops, network switches, and storage devices, making it easier for IT teams to know exactly what resources are available at any given time. This system also helps organizations keep track of software licenses, which is particularly important in preventing unlicensed software usage, ensuring compliance with vendor agreements, and avoiding potential legal or financial penalties. By maintaining an up-to-date inventory, organizations can also gain visibility into software installations and versions, helping them manage upgrades and patches more efficiently.

Another key benefit of effective IT asset and inventory management is cost optimization. Hardware and software investments can be significant, and inefficient management of assets can lead to unnecessary purchases, redundant systems, or underutilized resources. By maintaining a detailed inventory, organizations can identify unused or underutilized assets, which can either be reassigned to other departments or decommissioned to free up space and reduce costs. Additionally, asset management systems can track the depreciation of assets, allowing organizations to accurately assess their value over time and plan for replacement or upgrades. Through this process, businesses can reduce waste, extend the life of assets, and ensure that their technology investments deliver the maximum possible value.

Effective asset management also plays a crucial role in security and compliance. The management of IT assets is directly related to an organization's security posture. For example, organizations that do not track their hardware and software may face significant security risks. Untracked assets can lead to unauthorized devices being connected to the network, creating potential vulnerabilities. Similarly, using outdated or unpatched software can leave systems open to attacks. By keeping a comprehensive record of all assets and ensuring they are properly configured and maintained, businesses can better enforce security policies and ensure that their systems are compliant with industry regulations. For example, ITAM tools can help verify that only authorized devices are connected to the corporate network, that all devices are properly secured, and that software installations are in line with license agreements.

An increasingly important aspect of managing IT assets and inventory is sustainability. Organizations are under growing pressure to reduce their environmental impact, and IT asset management plays a key role in this effort. Proper disposal of outdated IT equipment, such as computers, servers, and networking devices, helps ensure that they do not contribute to electronic waste (e-waste). Many businesses are now adopting responsible disposal practices by partnering with certified e-waste recycling companies that safely recycle or repurpose old equipment. Additionally, organizations can use asset management data to make more informed decisions about purchasing more energy-efficient hardware, which can reduce electricity consumption and lower operating costs. As businesses strive to meet environmental goals, effective management of IT assets and inventory can contribute to these sustainability efforts.

Automation has increasingly become a key enabler of efficient asset and inventory management. Manual tracking of IT assets can be time-consuming and prone to errors, especially in large organizations with hundreds or thousands of assets. By automating asset tracking through technologies like barcode scanning, RFID, and integrated software solutions, businesses can significantly reduce administrative overhead. Automated systems can also provide real-time updates on asset status, location, and performance, which helps IT teams make quicker decisions and reduce downtime. Automation also helps in maintaining accurate records of assets, which is essential for audits, compliance, and lifecycle management.

In addition to automation, integration with other IT management systems is crucial for effective asset management. IT asset management tools should integrate with other systems, such as network monitoring, procurement, financial management, and incident management tools. This integration allows for a more comprehensive view of the organization's infrastructure, enabling IT teams to manage not just physical assets but also virtual assets, such as cloud resources and licenses, in a unified system. This creates a more holistic approach to IT infrastructure management, helping businesses optimize performance, reduce costs, and maintain better control over their entire technology environment.

Another important area that ties into IT asset and inventory management is risk management. Organizations must ensure that critical IT assets are covered by appropriate insurance and warranties. By having an accurate inventory of all assets, businesses can ensure that they are not underinsured or over-insured and that their policies are up to date. Furthermore, asset management helps businesses identify which assets are most critical to operations and prioritize their protection. This is particularly important in industries where downtime or data loss could have significant financial or regulatory consequences.

Managing IT assets and inventory is a critical function for businesses to maintain operational efficiency, security, and cost-effectiveness. With proper tracking, monitoring, and management of hardware, software, and network components, organizations can ensure that their IT resources are used optimally and that they are compliant with regulations. As organizations continue to expand and rely more heavily on technology, the importance of effective asset management will only grow, helping businesses stay competitive and ensure that their IT infrastructure supports their strategic goals. Through automation, integration, and responsible lifecycle management, companies can maximize the value of their IT investments while minimizing risks and costs.

Chapter 48: Scaling IT Infrastructure to Meet Growing Demands

As businesses expand and technology evolves, scaling IT infrastructure to meet growing demands has become a critical challenge for organizations of all sizes. The need for scalability arises from various factors, including increased data volumes, user traffic, new business requirements, and the growing complexity of applications. Scaling IT infrastructure effectively ensures that businesses can continue to operate smoothly, deliver services to customers, and stay competitive in a rapidly changing environment. The process of scaling involves adding resources, whether computing power, storage, or network capacity, in a way that aligns with organizational goals, maintains system performance, and avoids unnecessary expenditures.

Scaling IT infrastructure can be broken down into two primary approaches: vertical scaling and horizontal scaling. Vertical scaling, also known as "scaling up," involves adding more resources to a single machine, such as increasing the processing power, memory, or storage of an existing server. This approach is typically easier to implement and manage because it involves upgrading or adding components to an already existing infrastructure. However, vertical scaling has its limits; there is a point where a single server or machine can no longer support further upgrades without significant cost or performance degradation. It is generally more suited for situations where growth is predictable, and demand does not outstrip the capabilities of existing systems.

On the other hand, horizontal scaling or "scaling out" involves adding more machines or servers to a network to distribute the load and increase capacity. This approach is more flexible and allows businesses to scale infrastructure in a more dynamic way, adding resources as demand increases. Horizontal scaling is essential in cloud environments and large-scale data centers, where the volume of traffic and data can grow unpredictably. By distributing workloads across multiple servers or nodes, businesses can ensure better load balancing, fault tolerance, and redundancy. Horizontal scaling is often preferred for applications that require high availability and can be scaled independently, such as web servers or distributed databases.

One of the key benefits of scaling IT infrastructure is improved performance. As demand for services grows, so does the load placed on IT systems. Without scaling, systems can become overloaded, resulting in slow performance, increased latency, or even system failures. By adding more resources or distributing the load across multiple servers, businesses can ensure that their infrastructure remains responsive and can handle increased traffic. This is particularly important for businesses with customer-facing applications, where performance is critical for user experience and satisfaction. As websites, online platforms, and applications see increased traffic, scaling ensures that performance remains consistent and that the infrastructure can accommodate peak loads.

Cloud computing has revolutionized how organizations scale their IT infrastructure. The flexibility and on-demand nature of cloud services make it easier for businesses to scale their infrastructure without the need for heavy upfront investments in physical hardware. Cloud service providers such as Amazon Web Services (AWS), Microsoft Azure, and Google Cloud offer a range of services that allow businesses to scale resources up or down as needed. The cloud enables organizations to leverage virtual machines, storage, and other services on a pay-as-you-go basis, meaning businesses only pay for what they use, making it a cost-effective option for scaling.

In addition to the flexibility of cloud environments, cloud providers offer built-in tools for automated scaling, allowing businesses to dynamically adjust their infrastructure based on real-time usage. For example, if a web application experiences a surge in traffic, the cloud platform can automatically provision additional servers to handle the load and scale down when demand decreases. This automation ensures that businesses can respond quickly to changes in demand, without requiring manual intervention, which is especially useful for businesses with fluctuating traffic patterns or seasonal spikes in usage.

Another important factor in scaling IT infrastructure is load balancing. As organizations scale horizontally, they must ensure that workloads are distributed efficiently across the available resources. Load balancers are used to distribute incoming traffic evenly across multiple servers, ensuring that no single server becomes overwhelmed with requests. By using load balancing, businesses can achieve higher availability and reliability, as the failure of one server does not impact the overall performance of the system. Load balancing also improves response times by ensuring that traffic is routed to the least busy server, optimizing resource usage and reducing latency.

Scaling IT infrastructure also requires careful consideration of storage needs. As businesses generate more data, the demand for storage capacity increases. Traditional storage systems, such as direct-attached storage (DAS), may not be sufficient to handle large-scale data requirements, which is why businesses are increasingly adopting cloud storage solutions or distributed file systems. These technologies allow businesses to scale their storage needs easily and cost-effectively, without having to manage physical storage devices. Cloud storage solutions also offer the advantage of being accessible from anywhere, which is critical for businesses with remote teams or those that require high availability and disaster recovery capabilities.

The need for security also grows as IT infrastructure scales. Larger systems are more complex and may have more entry points for potential attackers. As businesses scale their infrastructure, they must ensure that security measures such as firewalls, encryption, and access controls are in place to protect sensitive data and systems. Scalable security solutions, such as distributed firewalls and intrusion detection systems, are essential to ensure that systems remain secure as they grow. In cloud environments, businesses must also ensure that their cloud providers have the necessary security certifications and that they adhere to industry-specific regulations, such as GDPR or HIPAA, to ensure compliance.

Cost management is another important consideration when scaling IT infrastructure. While scaling provides many benefits, it can also lead to significant costs if not managed properly. Cloud-based solutions, for example, allow businesses to scale resources dynamically, but if not monitored, they can result in unexpected charges. It is crucial for businesses to have a clear understanding of their infrastructure requirements and to use cost management tools provided by cloud providers to monitor usage and optimize spending. This includes setting budgets, tracking resource utilization, and taking advantage of pricing models that provide discounts for long-term commitments or reserved instances.

Automation plays a vital role in scaling IT infrastructure effectively. As organizations grow, the manual processes involved in scaling infrastructure, such as provisioning servers, configuring networks, or deploying applications, can become cumbersome and error-prone. Automation tools, such as infrastructure as code (IaC), allow businesses to define and manage their infrastructure using code, making it easier to scale quickly and consistently. IaC tools like Terraform, Ansible, and AWS CloudFormation allow organizations to automate the deployment and configuration of their infrastructure, ensuring that scaling operations are efficient, repeatable, and less prone to human error.

In an increasingly digital world, businesses must be prepared to scale their IT infrastructure to meet growing demands. Whether through vertical or horizontal scaling, cloud computing, automation, or enhanced security measures, scaling is essential for ensuring that IT resources are available and performing optimally as businesses grow. Properly scaled infrastructure ensures that organizations can handle increased workloads, support new applications, and provide reliable services to customers. As technology continues to evolve, the ability to scale IT infrastructure will remain a key factor in maintaining competitiveness, operational efficiency, and overall business success.

Chapter 49: Future Trends in IT Infrastructure: AI and Machine Learning

As businesses and organizations continue to evolve, the integration of artificial intelligence (AI) and machine learning (ML) into IT infrastructure is becoming increasingly significant. These technologies are not just shaping the way organizations interact with data but are also driving the transformation of how IT systems are designed, optimized, and managed. The future of IT infrastructure lies in the seamless incorporation of AI and ML, creating smarter, more efficient systems that can predict, adapt, and optimize performance autonomously. As businesses strive for greater agility, cost efficiency, and innovation, AI and ML are positioned to become the backbone of next-generation IT infrastructures.

The role of AI and machine learning in IT infrastructure goes far beyond the automation of routine tasks. Traditionally, IT infrastructure management involved manual monitoring, troubleshooting, and optimization. However, as systems grow in complexity and scale, the need for intelligent, adaptive solutions has become apparent. AI and ML technologies enable IT systems to not only automate repetitive processes but also to learn from data and make decisions based on patterns and insights that would be impossible for humans to detect in real time. This transformative capability is revolutionizing areas like system monitoring, performance optimization, and predictive maintenance.

In system monitoring, AI and ML are already being used to automate the process of detecting anomalies and potential system failures. Traditionally, IT teams rely on monitoring tools that track a variety of metrics, such as CPU usage, memory consumption, and network traffic, to ensure that systems are operating efficiently. However, these tools can only alert administrators when thresholds are crossed, often after the damage has already been done. AI-powered monitoring solutions, on the other hand, can analyze vast amounts of data from multiple sources in real time, identifying not only when a threshold has been exceeded but also predicting when problems might arise. By analyzing historical performance data and recognizing patterns, AI can anticipate failures before they occur, allowing for proactive maintenance and avoiding costly downtime.

In the realm of performance optimization, AI and ML technologies are poised to dramatically improve the way IT infrastructure is managed. Traditional performance optimization requires IT teams to manually tweak systems and applications based on a set of predefined rules. However, AI-driven systems can optimize performance autonomously by learning from data and adjusting resources based on usage patterns.

For example, cloud environments can use machine learning algorithms to allocate resources dynamically based on demand, ensuring that workloads are always running efficiently without over-provisioning or underutilizing resources. This can lead to substantial cost savings as organizations are only using the computing power they need at any given time.

Another area where AI and ML are making an impact is in predictive maintenance. Maintaining IT infrastructure often involves routine checks and preventative measures to ensure that systems are running smoothly. However, the cost and time involved in proactive maintenance can be significant, and sometimes systems fail unexpectedly despite regular checks. AI and ML can help organizations shift from reactive to predictive maintenance by analyzing data from sensors, logs, and other sources to detect early signs of hardware or software degradation. Machine learning models can identify subtle patterns in this data that indicate a potential failure, enabling IT teams to address issues before they lead to downtime or service interruptions. This predictive capability helps organizations extend the life of their equipment and minimize disruptions to business operations.

In terms of security, AI and ML technologies are becoming essential in protecting IT infrastructure against evolving cyber threats. Traditional security systems rely on predefined signatures and rules to identify potential security breaches, but these approaches are often insufficient against sophisticated and constantly changing cyberattacks. AI-driven security solutions can analyze vast amounts of data from multiple sources, including network traffic, user behavior, and system logs, to identify unusual patterns that may indicate a security breach. Machine learning models can continuously adapt and improve their ability to detect new threats, providing more effective and adaptive defense mechanisms. AI-based security systems are also capable of automating the response to security incidents, such as blocking suspicious traffic or isolating compromised systems, thus reducing the time it takes to mitigate threats.

One of the most exciting areas where AI and ML are impacting IT infrastructure is in network management. Network infrastructure is becoming more complex as businesses adopt hybrid cloud environments, edge computing, and a greater number of connected devices. Managing these networks manually is increasingly difficult, particularly when it comes to ensuring optimal performance, security, and reliability. AI and ML can be used to automate network configuration, monitoring, and troubleshooting, providing real-time insights into network health and automatically adjusting settings based on usage patterns. For instance, AI algorithms can be used to dynamically route traffic through the most efficient paths, ensuring faster data transmission and reducing latency. Machine learning can also be employed to predict network congestion, allowing for proactive adjustments before performance is impacted.

Cloud infrastructure is also benefiting significantly from the integration of AI and ML. As organizations continue to migrate to the cloud, managing and optimizing cloud resources becomes an increasingly complex task. AI and ML technologies enable cloud optimization by analyzing usage patterns and predicting future demand. For example, cloud service providers can use machine learning models to automatically adjust resource allocation based on real-time data, ensuring that businesses have the necessary computing power when they need it, without overpaying for unused capacity. This dynamic allocation helps optimize costs while maintaining performance and scalability, which is essential in a cloud-first world.

As AI and ML technologies continue to mature, they will play a central role in driving self-healing infrastructures. The concept of self-healing involves the ability of a system to automatically detect and correct issues without human intervention. AI-driven systems can monitor infrastructure components, detect performance degradation, and automatically take corrective actions, such as restarting services, reallocating resources, or patching vulnerabilities. This level of automation not only reduces the need for manual intervention but also enhances the resilience and reliability of IT systems. Businesses can rely on self-healing systems to ensure that their infrastructure remains operational even during unexpected failures, minimizing downtime and reducing the risk of human error.

The integration of AI and ML into IT infrastructure also raises new challenges and considerations. While these technologies offer numerous benefits, they also require businesses to invest in specialized skills, tools, and processes to fully realize their potential. For example,

IT teams need to be trained in machine learning algorithms and AI-driven tools to effectively manage these systems. Additionally, organizations must ensure that their data is clean, well-organized, and available for machine learning models to function effectively. There are also ethical and privacy concerns related to the use of AI, particularly in the context of data collection and decision-making. Businesses must ensure that their AI systems are transparent, explainable, and comply with regulations such as GDPR to maintain trust and avoid legal issues.

As AI and ML continue to shape the future of IT infrastructure, their impact will be felt across every layer of technology, from hardware to software to security. By harnessing the power of AI and ML, organizations can create more efficient, secure, and resilient IT systems that are better equipped to handle the demands of an increasingly digital world. As these technologies evolve, businesses will have the opportunity to transform their infrastructure management practices, paving the way for greater agility, scalability, and innovation.

Chapter 50: Sustainability in IT Infrastructure

Sustainability in IT infrastructure is becoming an increasingly critical concern as organizations face growing pressure to reduce their environmental impact while maintaining operational efficiency. As the demand for data, computing power, and digital services continues to rise, IT systems, which rely heavily on energy-consuming data centers, networks, and devices, contribute significantly to global energy consumption and carbon emissions. Consequently, integrating sustainable practices into IT infrastructure management has become essential not only for minimizing environmental impact but also for aligning with corporate social responsibility (CSR) goals, improving operational efficiency, and meeting regulatory requirements. This chapter explores the importance of sustainability in IT infrastructure and highlights the strategies organizations can adopt to reduce their environmental footprint while supporting long-term business goals.

The first step towards achieving sustainability in IT infrastructure is understanding the environmental impact of various components. Data centers are the cornerstone of most IT infrastructures, and they consume substantial amounts of energy to power servers, storage systems, and networking equipment. In addition to energy consumption, the cooling systems required to maintain optimal operating temperatures in data centers also contribute to significant environmental impact. The energy used in data centers is primarily derived from electricity, and depending on the source of this electricity, it can lead to increased carbon emissions. In regions where the grid relies heavily on fossil fuels, data centers can become substantial contributors to an organization's carbon footprint. This makes it crucial for businesses to assess the sustainability of their data centers and work towards reducing their energy usage, improving energy efficiency, and utilizing renewable energy sources.

One of the most effective ways to promote sustainability in IT infrastructure is through energy efficiency. Organizations can reduce their energy consumption by adopting energy-efficient hardware and optimizing their systems for better power management. Modern servers, storage devices, and networking equipment are designed to consume less power while delivering the required performance. Additionally, businesses can optimize the use of their infrastructure by consolidating workloads, reducing idle times, and leveraging virtualization technologies to maximize resource utilization. Virtualization allows multiple virtual machines to run on a single physical server, which reduces the number of physical devices required and, as a result, lowers the overall energy consumption of the infrastructure. IT teams can also implement power management features, such as automatic shutdowns or low-power states during off-peak hours, further reducing energy consumption.

Another approach to improving sustainability in IT infrastructure is the use of renewable energy. As part of their commitment to reducing their environmental impact, many organizations are transitioning to renewable energy sources to power their data centers and operations. Solar, wind, and hydroelectric power are some of the most common forms of renewable energy used by data centers and IT facilities. By sourcing their energy from these renewable sources, organizations can significantly reduce the carbon emissions associated with their IT infrastructure. Furthermore, some cloud providers have committed to using renewable energy for their data centers, making it easier for businesses to lower their carbon footprint by choosing cloud services that rely on sustainable energy. Organizations can also work with their utility providers to explore options for renewable energy purchasing or renewable energy credits (RECs) to further offset their environmental impact.

Green data centers are a key component of sustainable IT infrastructure. These data centers are designed with energy efficiency in mind and incorporate a range of environmentally friendly technologies and practices. For example, green data centers often use advanced cooling techniques, such as free cooling, which utilizes external air or water to cool the servers instead of traditional air conditioning. This reduces the amount of energy required for cooling and helps lower the overall environmental impact of the data center. Additionally, many green data centers are designed to be modular, allowing for easy scalability and efficient resource utilization. This modularity reduces the need for overbuilding, ensuring that energy is only used when necessary. Green building standards, such as LEED (Leadership in Energy and Environmental Design), are often applied to ensure that the construction and operation of data centers minimize their environmental impact.

Sustainability in IT infrastructure also extends to the lifecycle management of hardware and devices. The rapid pace of technological advancement means that IT hardware often becomes obsolete quickly, leading to increased electronic waste (e-waste). E-waste poses significant environmental challenges due to the toxic materials contained in electronic devices, such as lead, mercury, and cadmium. To mitigate the environmental impact of e-waste, organizations must adopt responsible disposal and recycling practices. This involves working with certified e-waste recycling companies that can safely handle and recycle old IT equipment. In addition, organizations can extend the lifespan of their IT equipment through refurbishing and reuse, which reduces the need for new devices and minimizes waste. Businesses should also consider purchasing energy-efficient devices and longer-lasting equipment that is designed for easier recycling at the end of its lifecycle.

Cloud computing plays a significant role in enhancing the sustainability of IT infrastructure. By leveraging the cloud, organizations can offload their IT infrastructure needs to cloud service providers that operate large-scale, energy-efficient data centers. Cloud providers are increasingly focusing on sustainability, with many investing in energy-efficient technologies and utilizing renewable energy to power their data centers. For businesses, this means they can access computing resources without the need to maintain their own physical servers, reducing energy consumption and hardware waste. Cloud-based infrastructure also allows for better scalability, ensuring that resources are used efficiently and only when needed. This pay-as-you-go model enables organizations to reduce the environmental impact of underutilized infrastructure, ensuring that they are not maintaining excess capacity or wasting resources.

In addition to focusing on energy efficiency and hardware management, organizations should also prioritize sustainable software development practices. Software applications can be optimized to reduce the energy consumption of the underlying hardware. Efficient software can perform the same tasks while requiring fewer resources, reducing the load on data centers and, in turn, lowering the environmental impact. For instance, businesses can optimize their applications for better performance, ensuring that they are resource-efficient and do not unnecessarily strain hardware. Additionally, organizations can adopt green coding practices that minimize energy consumption by reducing the complexity of algorithms and leveraging more efficient programming techniques.

Finally, sustainability reporting and tracking play a crucial role in driving improvements in IT infrastructure sustainability. By measuring and tracking the energy usage, carbon emissions, and overall environmental impact of their IT operations, organizations can identify areas for improvement and set measurable sustainability goals. Regular reporting allows businesses to monitor their progress over time and adjust their strategies as needed. Many organizations now publish annual sustainability reports that highlight their efforts to reduce their environmental footprint, including the steps taken in IT infrastructure management. These reports help businesses demonstrate their commitment to sustainability and transparency, which can enhance their reputation among customers, investors, and stakeholders.

Sustainability in IT infrastructure is not just about reducing environmental impact but also about aligning with broader corporate values and improving operational efficiency. By adopting energy-efficient technologies, sourcing renewable energy, managing e-waste responsibly, and leveraging cloud services, organizations can reduce their carbon footprint while optimizing their IT resources. As businesses continue to prioritize sustainability, IT infrastructure will increasingly be at the forefront of driving innovation, resource efficiency, and environmental stewardship in the digital age.

Chapter 51: The Evolution of IT Infrastructure Technologies

The evolution of IT infrastructure technologies has dramatically transformed how organizations design, deploy, and manage their digital environments. From the early days of mainframe computers to the modern, highly distributed cloud infrastructures, IT infrastructure has continually evolved to meet the demands of increasing complexity, scalability, performance, and cost-effectiveness. This transformation has not only impacted how businesses operate but has also driven innovation in virtually every industry, enabling greater efficiency, connectivity, and access to resources. The history of IT infrastructure is characterized by key technological advancements that have reshaped how businesses and organizations manage their digital resources, resulting in a more flexible and dynamic approach to IT management.

In the early days of computing, IT infrastructure was built around mainframe computers, which were large, expensive machines capable of handling massive amounts of data processing. These systems were typically housed in centralized data centers and were accessed by users through terminals, often running simple applications. The centralized nature of mainframe computing meant that resources were limited, and users had to share the available computing power. This model was ideal for the time, as it provided a single point of control for managing resources. However, as technology advanced and the demands of businesses grew, the limitations of mainframe systems became increasingly apparent.

The next significant shift in IT infrastructure came with the advent of client-server computing, which began to emerge in the 1980s and 1990s. In this model, computing tasks were distributed between clients (such as personal computers or workstations) and servers (which housed and managed the data). This decentralization allowed businesses to scale their IT infrastructure more efficiently, as individual users could access servers for specific applications and data without needing to rely on a single, centralized system. The client-server model was a significant improvement over mainframe systems, as it allowed for more flexibility, improved performance, and better resource allocation. Additionally, the rise of personal computers in the workplace democratized computing, allowing users to have their own devices while still benefiting from shared server resources.

As businesses increasingly relied on digital technologies, the next major shift in IT infrastructure came with the rise of networking technologies and the expansion of the internet. In the late 1990s and early 2000s, the proliferation of the internet and networking technologies allowed for greater connectivity between systems, enabling businesses to move towards more distributed architectures. This period marked the transition from standalone systems to interconnected environments, where data could be shared seamlessly between devices across wide areas. Networking technologies such as Ethernet, TCP/IP, and wireless connectivity formed the backbone of this evolution, enabling businesses to create more flexible and scalable infrastructures that could support a growing number of users, applications, and devices.

As the internet and networking technologies continued to evolve, businesses began to embrace virtualization in the mid-2000s. Virtualization allowed organizations to run multiple virtual machines (VMs) on a single physical server, effectively maximizing the use of available resources and reducing hardware costs. This technology enabled businesses to create more dynamic and efficient IT environments by allowing them to allocate resources on-demand and scale infrastructure without the need for additional physical hardware.

Virtualization also improved flexibility by enabling the rapid provisioning and deployment of new servers, applications, and services. This capability proved essential for organizations as they increasingly moved towards more complex and dynamic computing environments, particularly with the rise of cloud computing.

The advent of cloud computing in the late 2000s marked another revolutionary shift in IT infrastructure. Cloud computing provided businesses with the ability to access computing resources such as storage, processing power, and networking on-demand, without the need to invest in and maintain their own physical infrastructure. Public cloud providers like Amazon Web Services (AWS), Microsoft Azure, and Google Cloud transformed the IT landscape by offering scalable, flexible, and cost-efficient solutions for businesses of all sizes. Cloud computing not only reduced the upfront capital expenditures associated with maintaining data centers and hardware but also allowed businesses to scale their operations quickly and efficiently. As cloud infrastructure grew in popularity, it became the foundation for many modern applications, providing businesses with access to a virtually limitless pool of resources that could be utilized as needed.

As the cloud computing model evolved, new technologies emerged to further enhance IT infrastructure capabilities. One such advancement was the rise of containerization and microservices. Containers, powered by technologies such as Docker, allowed businesses to package applications and their dependencies into lightweight, portable units that could run consistently across different environments. Containers provided a more efficient and flexible way to deploy applications compared to traditional virtual machines, as they shared the underlying host operating system and required fewer resources. This shift to containers paved the way for the adoption of microservices architectures, where applications were broken down into smaller, independent services that could be developed, deployed, and scaled independently. Together, containerization and microservices enabled businesses to build more agile, scalable, and resilient applications that could be deployed quickly and reliably in cloud environments.

Another key development in the evolution of IT infrastructure is the growing importance of edge computing. As the internet of things (IoT) and connected devices continue to proliferate, organizations are increasingly faced with the challenge of processing vast amounts of data generated at the edge of networks, such as from sensors, smart devices, and autonomous systems. Edge computing involves processing data closer to where it is generated, rather than relying on centralized cloud servers. By doing so, businesses can reduce latency, optimize bandwidth usage, and improve real-time decision-making. Edge computing is particularly critical for applications that require fast, low-latency responses, such as autonomous vehicles, industrial automation, and smart cities. The rise of edge computing is driving a new wave of infrastructure innovations, as businesses look to deploy distributed computing resources closer to the data source while maintaining centralized control and coordination.

The future of IT infrastructure is likely to be shaped by the continued convergence of AI and machine learning with infrastructure management. AI and ML have the potential to revolutionize how IT systems are designed, deployed, and maintained by enabling infrastructure to become more intelligent and self-optimizing. For instance, AI algorithms can be used to predict system failures before they occur, automate resource allocation based on real-time demand, and enhance security by identifying threats and anomalies. As AI and ML technologies mature, they will become increasingly integrated into IT infrastructure management tools, making it possible for systems to automatically adapt and optimize based on usage patterns and performance data.

The evolution of IT infrastructure technologies has been marked by continuous innovation, each phase providing more flexibility, scalability, and efficiency than the last. From the early days of mainframe computing to the current era of cloud, containers, edge computing, and AI-driven infrastructure, each advancement has brought new capabilities that allow businesses to meet the growing demands of an increasingly digital world. As technology continues to advance, IT infrastructures will become even more dynamic, intelligent, and interconnected, driving further innovation across industries and reshaping how organizations operate and deliver services.

Chapter 52: Conclusion: Building a Robust IT Infrastructure

Building a robust IT infrastructure is essential for organizations aiming to thrive in today's fast-paced and technologically-driven world. As businesses continue to expand and digital transformation accelerates, the role of a well-structured, reliable, and scalable IT infrastructure cannot be overstated. A solid IT foundation enables organizations to manage their operations efficiently, respond to customer needs quickly, and innovate in a highly competitive market. At the heart of this infrastructure lies the integration of hardware, software, networks, and data management systems, all of which must work harmoniously to support the business goals and adapt to future challenges. The complexity of building and maintaining such an infrastructure, however, requires careful planning, continuous assessment, and the adoption of emerging technologies that can enhance the overall efficiency and performance.

At the core of a resilient IT infrastructure is its scalability. As businesses grow and their needs evolve, infrastructure must be capable of expanding without compromising performance or reliability. Scalability involves not only the ability to add more resources— whether storage, processing power, or network capacity—but also to scale intelligently. Cloud computing has revolutionized scalability, allowing organizations to dynamically allocate resources based on demand. The flexibility that cloud platforms provide means that businesses no longer need to over-provision hardware or commit to costly long-term infrastructure investments. However, scaling an infrastructure goes beyond simply adding resources. It also requires sophisticated management practices to ensure that systems can grow without leading to inefficiencies or increased operational complexity. Balancing the growth of infrastructure with operational needs is an ongoing challenge that requires continual assessment and optimization.

A key factor in building a robust IT infrastructure is security. As the number of cyber threats continues to rise, protecting infrastructure from external attacks, data breaches, and internal vulnerabilities becomes critical. Security must be embedded at every layer of the infrastructure, from the physical hardware to the network and software applications. Ensuring that firewalls, encryption, access controls, and intrusion detection systems are in place is essential to safeguarding an organization's most valuable assets: its data and intellectual property. Security measures should not be static but instead evolve in response to emerging threats. A proactive approach to security, including regular vulnerability assessments and incident response plans, ensures that the infrastructure can withstand the constantly changing landscape of cyber risks.

Another crucial aspect of building a strong IT infrastructure is reliability. The infrastructure must be designed to ensure continuous uptime, even in the face of hardware failures, network issues, or unforeseen events. High availability and disaster recovery strategies play an essential role in ensuring that critical systems and data are accessible when needed. Redundancy, load balancing, and failover systems are important components of a reliable infrastructure, as they ensure that if one part of the system fails, another can take over seamlessly. Regular backups, both onsite and offsite, further ensure that data is protected and can be quickly restored in the event of a disaster. Businesses cannot afford to have their operations interrupted for extended periods, as downtime can lead to significant financial losses, damage to customer trust, and disruption of services. Therefore, building an infrastructure that can recover quickly from failures is a fundamental requirement.

Equally important in the creation of a robust IT infrastructure is performance optimization. In the digital age, the performance of IT systems directly affects the user experience and business outcomes. Slow or inefficient systems can lead to frustration, decreased productivity, and lost opportunities. Optimizing the performance of IT infrastructure involves ensuring that hardware and software are well-tuned, network traffic is properly managed, and resources are allocated efficiently. Virtualization and containerization technologies, for example, allow businesses to maximize their resources and ensure that applications run smoothly even under heavy workloads. Monitoring tools, performance analytics, and automated scaling mechanisms all play a part in maintaining optimal performance levels. Continuous monitoring helps detect issues before they affect users, allowing for proactive intervention to maintain high performance.

The integration of emerging technologies into IT infrastructure is another significant factor in building a future-proof system. The digital landscape is constantly evolving, and businesses must ensure that their infrastructure can keep pace with technological advancements. AI, machine learning, edge computing, and blockchain are just a few of the innovations that are shaping the future of IT infrastructure. These technologies offer new ways to optimize operations, enhance security, and improve efficiency. For example, AI and machine learning can be integrated into infrastructure management tools to predict failures, optimize resource allocation, and improve decision-making. Edge computing is driving the need for more decentralized infrastructure, as data is processed closer to the source, reducing latency and improving responsiveness. Embracing these innovations allows businesses to stay competitive and agile in a constantly changing environment.

Sustainability is also becoming an increasingly important factor in IT infrastructure design. Organizations are under growing pressure to reduce their carbon footprint and minimize their environmental impact. This includes adopting energy-efficient hardware, leveraging renewable energy sources for data centers, and reducing e-waste through responsible disposal and recycling practices. Green computing initiatives, such as using energy-efficient cooling systems and optimizing power usage, are becoming integral parts of modern IT infrastructure. As businesses become more aware of their environmental responsibility, sustainable IT practices will play a significant role in infrastructure design, making it not only cost-effective but also environmentally friendly.

Building a robust IT infrastructure requires a deep understanding of an organization's goals, challenges, and future needs. It requires balancing a wide range of factors, including scalability, security, performance, reliability, and innovation. Organizations must be able to predict and respond to changes in demand, incorporate new technologies, and mitigate risks that could disrupt operations. This is an ongoing process that involves continuous assessment, adaptation, and improvement. The complexity of modern IT systems requires a collaborative approach, with cross-functional teams working together to design, implement, and manage infrastructure that meets business objectives. Successful IT infrastructure is not built overnight but evolves over time, adapting to the changing needs of the business and technological advancements.

In conclusion, building a robust IT infrastructure is essential for businesses to remain competitive and operate effectively in the digital era. It involves creating a flexible, secure, and reliable foundation that supports both current and future business needs. Organizations must prioritize scalability, performance, security, and sustainability in their infrastructure strategies, ensuring that their systems can support growth, adapt to new technologies, and withstand potential disruptions. By investing in the right technologies, practices, and frameworks, businesses can build IT infrastructures that enable them to thrive in an increasingly digital and interconnected world.